Sisters Listening to Sisters

Sisters Listening to Sisters

Women of the World Share Stories of Personal Empowerment

PEGGY ANDREWS

BERGIN & GARVEY

Westport, Connecticut • London

Library of Congress Cataloguing-in-Publication Data

Andrews, Peggy.
  Sisters listening to sisters : women of the world share stories of
personal empowerment / Peggy Andrews.
     p.   cm.
  Includes bibliographical references and index.
  ISBN 0–89789–475–8 (alk. paper).—ISBN 0–89789–476–6 (pbk. :
alk. paper)
  1. Women—Social conditions—Case studies. 2. Women—Economic
conditions—Case studies. I. Title.
HQ1154.A6857   1996
305.42—dc20   96–15355

British Library Cataloguing in Publication Data is available.

Library of Congress Catalog Card Number: 96–15355
ISBN: 0–89789–475–8
ISBN: 0–89789–476–6 (pbk.)

First published in 1996

Bergin & Garvey, 88 Post Road West, Westport, CT 06881
An imprint of Greenwood Publishing Group, Inc.

Printed in the United States of America

The paper used in this book complies with the
Permanent Paper Standard issued by the National
Information Standards Organization (Z39.48–1984).

10 9 8 7 6 5 4 3 2 1

To My Mother

Christina M. Schroeder Andrews

My mother taught me to be a storyteller, I just didn't realize it until I was old enough to be retired. Now, I said, "old enough to be retired," not "retired." I don't think I ever will be retired.

Of course, she taught me many things but there are two things specially related to this book. She taught me to love people and to love travel. Now, she didn't set out to teach me any of these things, she just taught them because of who she was: a storyteller, a lover of people, and a lover of travel. She had a saying that was pretty much the essence of her love of travel: *The only time I get carsick is when the car goes without me.* In the 1940s when the song *Far Away Places* was popular, she called it her theme song. I am my mother's true daughter, at least when it comes to the love of travel.

Mother died before she was able to visit any of those Far Away Places, but she traveled to them with me. I saw the women through her eyes, listened to their stories through her ears; it was her love mixed with mine that reached out to the women. Mother, this book is for you. Thanks for teaching me and for being my traveling companion.

Contents

PART IV. RELIGIONS: OPPRESSIVE OR LIBERATING?

Preface

For the last fifteen years I have lived and traveled in twenty-seven countries, talking with and listening to women. I have learned about how their daily work is only completed after long hours of caring for the family, producing income, and serving the community and the joys they share among themselves. Some women told me stories of violence against women and their children. I was able to celebrate with sisters in their joys and grieve with them in sorrow.

My time in Zambia (1981–1984) as a teacher both with high-school girls at Njase Girls School and with college students at David Livingstone College provided me with many opportunities to travel in Zambia and to talk with and listen to women. While there, I was also able to travel to Kenya, Tanzania, Zimbabwe, and Botswana. I sought to learn from women in these countries about their lives, the lives of their families, and about their homelands.

On my way back to the United States I traveled in India, Thailand, Singapore, Hong Kong, and Taiwan. I met women who were street vendors in the *Shanti* garden in Madras, India; mothers in a Thailand village who told me why they had to sell their daughters into prostitution; mothers in Taiwan telling me about their daughters who work in the free-trade-zone factories in Taipei.

My travels to Mexico, Guatemala, El Salvador, Nicaragua, Costa Rica, and Cuba again gave me opportunities to listen to my sisters from that part of the globe. The women in the villages and cities shared their stories; and the richness of their lives empowered me. I listened to women who were doctors, professors, teachers, nurses, farmers, marketeers, small businesswomen, and in government. I also listened to women at international meetings and gatherings, in dialogue and conversation, and in books.

I heard these women of the world speak of pain and prophecy, sadness and suffering, humiliation and hope, freedom and faith, and liberation and love of life. The listening helped to bring understanding about their lives and the understanding has empowered me. I knew the women in the villages in Zambia, or in Tanzania, or in Thailand, or in Taiwan, or in Guatemala, or in El Salvador would not individually be able to tell their stories to the world, but they told their stories to me. Now I share them.

My hope for this book is that as you read their stories, you will come to know them: Beauty, Alicia, Vibhuti, Zellda, and all the others. In knowing them you will understand them; and in understanding you will become sisters with them. Our sameness gives us a starting point; our differences give us a rich fabric woven with the threads of our lives and embroidered with the beauty that we share as women—as sisters.

I am reminded of what my friend Frank Waters says in his introduction to *The Earp Brothers of Tombstone*. He quotes Mrs. Virgil Earp, "Now boy, you put some Fleischmann's Yeast in this and raise it up. You're just gettin' the facts now."[1] The women have given me their facts, their stories, and I have put some Fleishmann's Yeast in and let them raise up. Many of the names have been changed and some of the stories are composes of many women's stories. Not all the stories are pretty and not all the endings are happy. But the growth and strength in each teller and each listener is a beauty in itself. Know that each story is a part of that woman's life and the life of her family, community, and sometimes her country. But most of all, know that each story is a part of your life also. Many times I had to stop typing and dry my eyes. Remembering can be hard.

This was not an easy book but it was a book that I knew I had to write. Let the women's stories empower you as they have empowered me. Let our sisters' empowerment become part of your empowerment.

Some may call this a radical feminist book (I would be honored if they did). I think Elisabeth Schussler Fiorenza said it quite well: "Radical feminism has rediscovered the 'equality from below.'"[2] Empowering women is rediscovering equality.

Acknowledgments

My first and foremost thanks goes to the women around the world who have shared stories from the richness of their lives with me thus helping me to understand global sisterhood. My heartfelt thanks goes to the women and men who helped me meet our sisters whose stories are told here; without them I would not have been able to listen and learn. The privilege of meeting and the blessings from listening to the women are unmeasurable.

Over the years I have had the support and encouragement of many, many friends, too numerous to count, and more than any one person deserves. But there is one that I have to name, Frank Waters. He has been a mentor, an adopted father, and friend. His spirit in his eagle feather has hung over my head each day as I write.

I want to thank the following women, who read parts or all of the manuscript, for their valuable critiquing and for sending the copy back with a good case of the red mark "measles": Jean Barker, Deonne Barkley, Barbara Brandt, Sydney Brown, Betty Brunett, Sunie Clarke, Marilyn Chilcote, Martha DeWarf, Eleanor Durst, Helen Engeseth, Muriel Follansbee, Virginia Hadsell, Donna C. Kamper, June Klar, Alice Nishi, Mary Jane Patterson, Virginia Stowe, and Barbara Williams. A very special thanks goes to Judith Cunningham who is my friend, reader, prodder, and "jiminy cricket," and who also provided me with the opportunity to test out some of the stories in a seminar setting. She has been an invaluable support.

I want to thank the people at the information line at the Tucson-Pima Library for finding answers to my every question and need. A special thanks goes to Loretta A. Barrett for her encouragement to write the book and Lynn Flint for her help in starting me down the path of getting it published. I also want to thank my editors Nina Pearlstein, Maureen Melino, and Jodie McCune for all of their patience with this novice.

My deepest thanks goes to my three sons, Allan, Charles, and Clifford for their love for and confidence in me as I took on this new venture in life.

Sisters Listening to Sisters

1

Women Empowering Women

As women, we have a common gender identity that is not distorted or broken by geographic distance or historical background. Kathleen Fischer reflects in *Women at the Well*: "We are linked not only physically, but spiritually as well, to our mothers, our grandmothers, and all the women who have come before us. With them we share a common gender identity and the social roles and expectations that go with it."[1] It is this common gender identity that I hope to reinforce as we hear the stories of our sisters in developing countries and in the United States. The opportunity to empower each other is limited only by our own imaginations and lack of involvement.

Emily, one of my friends in Zambia, told me she felt that women represented what life was really like in her country. "If you want to know Zambia, get to know the women. The problems we face each day are the real problems of this country. The joys we have and the life we celebrate are the joys and life of Zambia."

One weekend, while Emily and I were visiting her home village, she showed me the well her grandfather had dug. She told me the story about how her grandmother's accident got her a well.

"My grandmother broke her leg when all of the children were gone from home to boarding school. Grandmother had been walking three kilometers each day for years carrying water for the family. Once my grandfather had to carry the water, he soon decided he needed to dig a well. My grandmother used to say that was the best accident she ever had." Emily's village proceeded to grew up around the well; when her grandfather had dug the well, the other huts in the area were scattered.

Emily's story reminds us that in historical times as well as today the toil and work of women is not recognized as valued work. The value of women has for the most part been measured by men. Now, in all parts of the world we can find women who are taking into their own hands how they will be valued—be viewed. In response many voices in developing countries are crying that the feminist movement is being imposed on their country. But few of those voices are women's voices.

One day I attended a political gathering for U.S. Ambassador Nicholas Platt at the soccer stadium in Choma, the station town close to the school. A Zambian man in the crowd stood up and remarked, "We appreciate all of the development help that your country has sent us. We need U.S. dollars. But is there some way that you can stop all of those women's liberation ideas that are corrupting our women from coming into our country from your country?"

Before Ambassador Platt could respond, a woman stood up. She was wearing a colorful Zambian dress and matching head wrap made out of cloth that depicted women marching with a sign, "We Want Our Liberation Now!"[2] She shouted over a bull horn she had brought, "We do not depend on our sisters from the United States to tell us that we still need our own rights," she said. "We know from the way we are treated daily that we are not liberated." At that moment women stood up throughout the gathering and joined in chanting, "We Want Our Liberation Now! We Want Our Liberation Now!"

That evening I asked a friend, who was one of those who stood up, if the group had known that the man was going to say something about the feminist movement. She answered, "Yes, he is always talking that way and his wife told us he was going to question Ambassador Platt, so we decided that would be a good time to speak out. We wanted to let the ambassador and the community know how the women feel. We have been pretty quiet, but we know we have to become more vocal. Men are not going to make changes! We are going to have to make the changes ourselves."

Women know that they are valued less than men in all sectors of national life: economic, political, social, and cultural. They know that the brokers of power will never give up their power, so women around the world must learn how to empower themselves. Their empowerment will take on a very different face from that of the dominating, exploiting, oppressing, authoritative power of the present day brokers of power. Many women have learned their lessons of empowerment through the liberation of their countries from imperialistic colonialism. But liberation of the country usually does not mean the liberation of women—as we just saw in Zambia. In many cases women have set aside their needs for the "larger" need of the country's liberation, from colonialism, but then found the needs of the country–health care, schooling, jobs, social services were their needs but were not being addressed. It is through the empowerment of women that these basic needs will be met.

The great UN Decade of Development (1960s) fizzled like a bad Roman candle on the Fourth of July. It got off the ground, then went "bang" and fell. It is only now after three decades of wondering what happened that the leaders of the international community are realizing that to sustain development they must begin

with "equality from below," with women, because it is women who have more
to do with the economy of the family and the community than men. The international
community is beginning to look at sustainable development as development that
allows the present population to meet their needs of livelihood while at the same
time sustaining the resources of the planet for future generations.

The "below" is no better illustrated than by the women who have no political
power, no vote, no economic power, and who are the social outcasts both in their
culture and their religious communities: *Harijans*, the untouchables of India. Yet
these women are finding their power—becoming empowered—through cooperation,
compassion, consensus, community, and competence.

A Gandhian feminist woman street vendor in Madras told of how she and several
other women, after meeting and talking several times, decided that if they worked
together, each selling different things instead of competing by trying to sell the
same things, they all would make more money. She told me, "It takes time to
build up trust and come to agreements, but we all knew we had to work together
if we were going to make any kind of gains in our lives." She told of improvements
they had made in their community. "We now have a school for our daughters,
a nurse comes once a week with medicine to keep people from getting sick, and
soon we hope to have water stand-pipes."

In the 1970s, women in the United States, realized that women's best interests
were also the best interests of the poorest, the oppressed and despised, as well
as the abused woman in the world. They knew no woman would be free until
every woman was free. Our sisters around the world were also saying the same
thing in the 1980s. The women working with the Asian Immigrant Women Advocacy
in Oakland, California, in the 1990s, know this is still true as they work for the
women garment workers in the Bay Area.

When we talk about empowerment, we are talking about women working together,
having a say about and control over our lives. Women around the world are doing
just that, but with a whole new kind of power—a power that comes from within.

Devaki Jain, a Gandhian feminist, sets forth five reflections women worldwide
seem to hold in common:

1. A desire for peace, reflecting the a rejection of the arms race by
   women.

2. Caring for others—family, community, and survival of the world
   ecologically.

3. Rejection of hierarchy and the use of cooperation as opposed to
   competition as a way of structuring society.

4. The capacity for self-reliance.[3] This can be found in urban and rural
   women, women of various classes, and women of all levels of
   education.

5.   There is a sense of tradition. Women are rooted in, and carriers of, cultural and religious traditions. Traditions can give women strength and a way of networking, but, it also can be the cause of much pain and oppression.[4]

It is within her Hindu tradition that Jain finds a basis for the feminist ethic. She realizes that religious structures often hinder those dynamics of liberation she feels all religious traditions have. Yet, she asserts that women must "move . . . beyond the establishment into freedom."[5] Jain asks the question, "Can we [women] find a philosophical, moral and ideological base for a feminist ethic?"[6]

Jain's concept of a feminist ethic is seen as empowering women throughout the world. Our methods of empowering ourselves need to be there tugging at us as we assume our leadership roles in our families, communities, nations, and world.

You will hear more later about Nawal el Saadawi, a Muslim Egyptian doctor, but now let's think about what she has to say about women's rights and about encouraging women: "We begin with change as individuals."[7] Saadawi continues that individuals can build solidarity and a power base at all levels: home, community, country, and international. An example is the pan-Arab association for women's rights, "The Association of Solidarity Between Women." Saadawi stresses, "Women must be able to see the linkages—between the oppression in the bedroom, in the nation, and on the international scene—and must work together to generate power."[8]

This empowerment that emerges from within has a different structure than when it comes from tradition. It is both horizontal and circular. When it moves up, it moves in a spiral, including the wholeness of life. This power uses cooperation, consensus, and critical analysis as a model. We find compassion and companionship, community and communion, in the way that women structure this power. This feminine power comes from a basis of equality. It does not seek to put women over men nor to insist that they have the same powers as men. It seeks a whole new power structure. This is radical feminism. Women around the world are seeing that the existing power structures are not meeting the needs of women, children, or the community. Instead they are looking within themselves and finding the power to change their lives and the lives of their children and their communities.

Their stories are beautiful stories. Some are not so pretty, but the women and their struggles to empower themselves are always beautiful. Listen, listen with your ears to their joys and their sorrows. Listen with your hearts to their gladness and suffering. But most of all listen with your being, to their being, and become one with them. Become sisters.

PART I

WOMEN EMPOWERING WOMEN ECONOMICALLY

2

How It All Works

As I traveled through developing countries, it was exciting to discover the ways women empower themselves economically. Women come together collectively to advocate for equal pay, safer working conditions, and health regulations. They work in community to obtain credit resources, they participate cooperatively in generating income, and they use consensus to get the job done. This is all the more exciting because these women face an environment that is traditionally hostile, that does not value women's contribution to the national or global economy.

RECOGNIZING WOMEN'S ECONOMIC ROLES

As we look at the development of the global economy we need to ask, "What economic roles do women have?" It is discouraging to find that national governments and international agencies include only the paid employment that women do when figuring the Gross National Product (GNP). Economists do not include either the work of women in the informal sector—such as women who are street vendors, subsistence farmers, or cottage industry workers—or women's unpaid work in caring for and producing goods and services for home and family.

Although women see their productive and reproductive activities as integral parts of their role, mainstream economists make a distinction between these two kinds of work. "The lack of value of our work doesn't allow it to be part of the equation in determining the need for funding for development projects or the services of agencies, both national and international," related Berta, a rural/urban migrant woman from Dar es Salaam, Tanzania, who was studying at the women's training center at Morogoro, Tanzania. Women's productive work usually includes tasks such as crop and livestock production, handicrafts, marketing, and wage employment—activities that contribute financially to the family and the community.

Reproductive work includes activities such as fuel and water gathering, food preparation, child care, informal education, health care, and home maintenance. Women often put up to eighteen hours a day into productive and reproductive work, but only their wage-earning work is counted as part of their country's GNP.

Many women in developing countries are virtual (or de-facto) heads of households. "Our men go to the city to find work, leaving us here on the land to support the family. I haven't heard from my husband since he went to Dar es Salaam over a year ago," Joy, a Tanzanian mother of three, told me. "I have to do all the work on the land and take care of the children. When I came here I had to get my mother to come and stay with my children. Since my husband left me I have no way of supporting my children. Coming to this training school will help me to grow more crops and know how to market them. I will also be able to help the other women in my village. They are helping my mother take care of my children. I miss my family but I had to do this so we could live," Joy said with a mixture of joy and sadness in her eyes.

Because many women like Joy have been deserted, women as heads of households are becoming even more prevalent. Many husbands in developing countries are seeking employment in other parts of their home country or out of the country. Some are able to send back money but many of them do not, spending it on themselves instead. This puts the burden of providing for the family on the women. The numerous civil strife and cross-border conflicts that plague developing countries aggravate to this situation, as most of the world's refugees, including those within their own country, are women and children, and this population is increasing daily.

The role of women in development has long been seen as passive. "The menfolk think they know what we need and, therefore, give it to us. How can they know in Nairobi what we need here in Tumu Tumu?" asked one of the women who had gathered to meet with me as I visited villages on the slopes of Mt. Kenya with a friend from the Presbyterian Church of East Africa.

"If the people from the other countries want to help us, let them listen to us. We can tell them what we need to feed our children," another mother explained.

I had seen pictures of squatters camps around cities, but I don't think anything could have prepared me for the endless flow of shanties that flooded Nairobi's Mathare Valley from ridge to ridge. The social worker from the National Council of Churches of Kenya and I spent the day with the women at this camp. There was a nutrition center; a weaver shop, where cotton was carded, spun, and dyed before it was woven into beautiful cloth; and a multipurpose building that served as a clinic, school, and church.

One resident was only twenty-five years old, dark wrinkles ringed her sunken eyes, her body showed the signs of many births and long hours of work. She had brought her children to the nutrition center to eat. Wanda lamented, "Here we need standpipes for water. How do I mix the high protein meal they give me here at the nutrition center without safe water? My children get sick with this water."

"We here in the valley know that we have to work for what we have, but sometimes it is very hard to survive, let alone live, because we do not even have the basic things like food, water, sanitation, shelter, health care, or education for our children. It was hard in the rural area but I would go back if I had the money to get there, but I can't save enough from the little my husband makes so we can go back," Wanda sighed wearily.

The women I met in developing countries told me the same things: Listen to us, we know what we need and what needs to be done. We are the ones that work the long hours for our families—we know. Don't send people to tell us what to do. Send people to listen to what we need.

THE GAP GETS WIDER—WHY?

The history of economic development over the last three-and-a-half decades is characterized by a widening gap between the rich and the poor.[1] Starting in the 1960s, donor countries in the developed world (the North) were eager to get on board the development train. Developing countries in the developing world (the South) received large sums of money through both multilateral and bilateral agencies. UN agencies, the World Bank, and the International Monetary Fund (IMF) led the way in dispersing multilateral aid, often as loans. The U.S. State Department and Department of Defense were also big contributors, as were other major industrialized countries of the North. However, most of these programs dealt exclusively with national governments of the receiving countries and not with local governments or nongovernmental organizations. They typically funded very large projects that were often technically inappropriate for local and community needs, and whose focus was on large infrastructure projects that did not "trickle down" to the people. For example, roads to transport the export goods of transnational corporations (TNC) received funding, but roads to transport goods from the rural area to markets did not. People need clean drinking water and small-farm irrigation projects, yet large dams and hydroelectric plants to supply the needs of factories were financed by loans.

A woman from Ghana, who was in a community development training program in Zambia, emphasized this point to me. "With the help of a small loan from a church group, we were able to use the bamboo that we grew to make pipes. The pipes carried the water from a spring down to our garden plots, and water to drink, and for our livestock. We don't need big expensive diesel pumps that cost to run and keep up. What we need are ways to do things with what we have."

WE EAT BREAD NOT BOMBS

In many developing countries, the U.S. Department of Defense provided military aid under the rubric of fighting communism and maintaining political stability in the country. Often as not this aid went to supporting dictators such as President Ferdinand Marcos in the Philippines and General Augusto Pinochet Ugarte in Chile. The training of soldiers who led the death squads in many Latin American countries was also financed by the U.S. Department of Defense.

Archbishop Oscar A. Romero of El Salvador wrote in his diary regarding his February 17, 1980, letter to President Jimmy Carter of the United States:

> It is prompted by the proximate danger that military aid signifies for El Salvador and especially by the notion of special warfare, which consists in eliminating in murderous fashion all the endeavors of people's organizations under the pretext of fighting communism or terrorism. This type of warfare means to do away with not only the men directly responsible but with their whole families, which in this view are all poisoned by these terroristic ideas and must be eliminated. The danger is serious, and the letter is designed to beg the President of the United States not to provide military aid, which would mean great harm to our people, because it would be destined to snuff out many lives.[2]

Archbishop Romero was assassinated by military personnel on March 24, 1980. In all probability these men were given the orders by Roberto D'Aubuisson, trained by the U.S. military as documented by the U.S. State Department.

Six years later, I talked with women at the offices of the Mothers of the Disappeared an organization in El Salvador of relatives and friends of those who had disappeared. I saw the results of U.S. military aid on the lives of ordinary families. It is the mothers, wives, and sisters who search the roadways and dump sites for the mutilated corpses of their relatives. At the celebration of mass at Nuestra Senora de Los Angeles Church in Managua, Nicaragua, there is a ritual of chanting "*Presente*" after the calling of each name of a killed or disappeared person. During this ritual I came to realize that it is the women with their strained faces of sorrow who carry the torch of hope for the people in their struggle to determine their own destiny.

MONEY, MONEY, AND MORE MONEY

It is not only governments that bring economic inequities to women of developing countries. Transnational corporations (TNCs) are also responsible. With home offices in the North, TNCs have used their powers of finance, technology, and media control to determine the models used in development schemes. TNCs' primary goal is the maximization their own profits worldwide.

The financial maneuvering of TNCs has led to the global economic crisis today. Fernando Fajnzylber in his exhaustive study for the United Nations shows that "during the years 1957–1965 . . . the U.S.-based global corporations financed eighty-three percent of their Latin American investment locally, either from reinvested earnings or from local Latin American savings. (With) only about seventeen percent of U.S. investment during the period."[3] The percentages of money loaned by the banks of the host country for the operations of TNCs was greater than the percentage of money brought into the country by the TNCs. Argentine economist Aldo Ferrer points our that between 1965 and 1968, TNCs returned fifty-two percent of their profits to the United States, while seventy-eight percent of the money invested to generate that profit came from the host country.[4] Furthermore, many of the investments of TNCs have not been in new factories or equipment but in takeovers or buy-outs.

The continuation of these policies has had a profound impact on the developing countries. As to be expected, women are the hardest hit. "When money goes out of the country, we have less for education and basic health care," asserts a Taiwanese woman living in the mountain area of that island state. "Our daughters leave the villages to work in the free-trade zone[5] factories, hoping to make enough money to send back home. Their wages are so small that it takes all they make just to survive in Taipei," she said. "If it is not the big factory men, then, it is the corrupt local men who make all the money, it is not the workers. Our daughters also lose their culture and traditions when they move to the city. We don't want them to go but money seems to be very important to them. There is one thing that has helped, and that is the church is there helping them to have a sense of community."

When questioned about their methods, TNCs often claim it is better to send money back to the United States than to give it to the Swiss bank accounts of corrupt local businessmen. Yet many of the local businessmen, along with local government officials, are in the pockets of TNCs.[6] Crumbs from the corporate table are offered to the workers.

With Eastern Bloc countries moving toward a market economy, and with the privatization of major economic entities occurring in the southern hemisphere, there are five red flags of concern to look out for that may keep this process from benefiting the people of these countries. First, make sure that short-term revenue-bearing sales do not endanger the long-term efficiency of the nation's economy. This happens when a government monopoly is replaced by a private monopoly, for example, railroads, electricity, and telephones. Second, be certain that governments will provide the appropriate structure, such as antitrust regulation, but not a heavy hand in allowing corporations room to change. A distinct probability of corruption is present if open and competitive bidding is not allowed and if the report of the bidding is not available to the public.

Third, avoid "robbing Peter to pay Paul." One of the most common reasons for privatization is to sell public enterprises to cover budget deficits. This leads to a bankrupted future. Fourth, insist that the sales of shares in privatized ventures be widespread. This helps to achieve a balance between foreign and national shareholders and to protect the national interest.

The fifth consideration is that labor must be part of the implementation of the privatization process. Layoffs must be kept to a minimum to make sure privatization serves the public good. The decisions and processes of privatization are both politically and economically based and need to involve the people.

TECHNOLOGY: APPROPRIATE OR INAPPROPRIATE?

Another problem is the TNCs' control of technology. The technology of the North may be the key to their economic power, but when transported to developing countries that technology does not always work. I saw an example of this in Zambia, where in some places twenty-foot-high anthills with a sixty-foot base are so close together that only three would fit on a hectare (2.47 acres). Farmers plant maize (corn) on and between these anthills. A large farm tractor is not able to plow the sides of the anthills, nor to maneuver between them effectively. Yet a large British farm implement company came to this area and talked to the farmers, convincing them to buy a large tractor. Small tractors or rototillers were much more appropriate for the land, and the cost of operation and maintenance could be carried on much more easily by the farmers.

The importing of technology for industry has caused a "brain drain" in the developing countries of the South. At a September 1989 conference, Third World Debt Crisis: Global/Local Links, in Washington, DC, Anivaldo Padilha, a Brazilian economist from the Ecumenical Center for Documentation and Information, explained to me about "brain drain." When a TNC comes to our country, they encourage our scientists to work with them but the company does not allow the patents developed by our scientists to remain in our country. At other times they will send the scientist to the home country of the TNC to work in their labs. Such practices keep the patents in the company's home country, spending their research and development dollars there and not in the host country. They encourage the few scientists that the host country has to go to the company labs in the home country to do research, thus keeping new technology under the control of the TNCs, and the host country loses their scientists. The oil industry is one example. Because oil refining technology is controlled by major oil companies, Latin American countries were not able to develop their own research and be competitive in the refinement of their oil.

This technological dependence has a profound impact on the developing countries. Along with the severe drawbacks and inappropriateness of modern technology as controlled by TNCs, developing countries suffer job loss. Technology that requires fewer labor hours may bring in more profits for the shareholders, but it displaces workers and widens the gap between the rich and the poor.

ONE PICTURE SELLS A THOUSAND PRODUCTS

The role that TNCs play in media is also felt in developing countries. Radios and televisions scream commercials across the countryside and throughout the cities, and magazines and newspapers are smear with ads. The North's control of the media gives the TNCs free reign in advertising their products. Madison Avenue actively promotes consumption-oriented life styles in the developing countries. Corporate America seems to think that what is good for the goose here also must be good for the gander overseas. Thus Coca-Cola, Johnson & Johnson, Kellogg's, Kodak, ITT, and R. J. Reynolds are but a few who have joined the media mania. A "global shopping center" is the goal and fast becoming a reality.[7]

Financial capital, technology, and media control make up the foundation of the economic power of TNCs—a power that is growing stronger each year and impacting the development of the South.

DEVELOPMENT: JUST A TITLE

By the end of the UN Decade of Development (1960s), the unemployed of the world population had grown to sixty percent, thus causing less purchasing power and lower consumption of goods. In a World Bank survey, Irma Adelman and Cynthia Taft Morris found there was a substantial increase in income for the top five percent of the population, while the lowest forty percent become even poorer.[8] It became apparent that the dramatic economic growth of countries like Korea and Brazil was not reaching the people. President Emilio Médici of Brazil put it very clearly: "Brazil is doing well but the people are not."[9]

Dr. Robert Mabele, of the Economic Research Bureau of the University of Dar es Salaam, Tanzania, told me how the oil crisis had affected his country. "In the seventies we saw changes in the economy and more of the same. With the beginning of the oil crisis came the generating of petrodollars to be invested. Banks were eager to lend to the developing countries that could not afford the fuel costs. They were also there to finance the loan payments with floating interest rates tied to the value of the U.S. dollar."

"Wasn't it also at this time that trade protection in the North started to become a significant factor?" I asked.

"Yes, and that forced low prices on our exports and higher prices on our imports. Many countries had to turn to the International Monetary Fund (IMF) for money. They, in turn, required severe structural adjustments, which resulted in unemployment of government workers, elimination of subsides on commodities, and cutbacks in social services such as health care, education, and transportation. We had to devaluate our currency, which caused sky-rocketing prices."

At the Third World Debt Crisis: Global/Local Links conference in 1989, as delegates talked with representatives of the World Bank, I was reminded of what its former president, Robert McNamara, had to say about the prevailing development policies in 1972 and their impact on the world. "Projected to the end of the century—only a generation away—that means the people of the developed countries will be enjoying per capita incomes, in 1972 prices, of over $8,000 a year, while those masses of the poor (who by that time will total over two and one-quarter billion) will, on the average, receive less than $200 per capita, and some 800 million of these will receive less than $100."[10]

Part of the reason for these changes is the flow of money to the North from the South. Jack Nelson-Pallmeyer brings this point forcefully to our attention: "The recent massive drain of wealth from the South to the North is reminiscent of the colonial conquest. In 1989 alone, the people of developing countries sent $52 billion more in debt payments to developed countries in the North than their nations received in new credits."[11]

The 1980s brought on the worst recession in the developing countries since the 1930s, with Africa and Latin America most severely affected. Drought conditions in Africa added to the misery of the people. As the world economy becomes increasingly interdependent, it also becomes even more unequal in trading relations.

"Development" still means trying to make the old model of "giving to and doing for" work. The gap grows between the rich and the poor both of the North and South.

FREE TRADE FOR WHOM?

Formal trading blocs and economic coalitions had been around for many years, but it was not until the late 1970s that they started to become an important part of the global economy. They have taken on an interesting configuration. The European Common Market (ECM), with Germany and France leading the way while supporting small countries like Greece and Portugal, constituted one of the world's largest trading blocks.

Another economic bloc that carries tremendous power—and one with a particularly interesting configuration is that of the industrialized nations of United States, Canada, Japan, Great Britain, Germany, France, and Italy which make up the Group of 7. This group strongly influences decisions made by the General Agreement on Tariffs and Trade (GATT), the World Bank, and the International Monetary Fund (IMF). During its twentieth annual economic summit, in the summer of 1994, the Group of 7 invited the Russians to attend but did not grant them full participant privileges.

One of the most recent trading blocs is that formed by the North American Free Trade Agreement (NAFTA), which went into effect January 1, 1994. Its goal is to remove the trade restrictions between Canada, the United States, and Mexico, there by erasing the stark line between North and South. The 2,066 mile border between Mexico and the United States is the only place in the world where a developed nation touches a developing country.

It is not only the industrialized North that is looking at trading blocs. Both African and Latin American countries as well as nations in Asia are coming together to try to influence prices and trade negotiations. However, because they lack the financial power, they have not been as successful in having an impact on the North, although they have been able to increase trade among themselves.

International trade would seem to be an area that would not be of importance to women, yet while talking to women in the developing countries I found there was an enormous impact from it. For instance, when cash crops for export are grown on the best land and the peasants, mostly women, are marginalized to mountain slopes and rocky ravines, they often are unable to grow enough to feed themselves. As a result, these countries have less locally grown food to sell in the cities, and imported food is too expensive to be part of their daily diet.

"The taking of our crop land to grow tobacco for export cuts down our maize production. The government imported yellow corn for us to eat. Yellow corn is for livestock feed, not for us to eat. We eat white mealie-meal. Yellow nshima[12] is not part of our diet," explained Shirley, a home economist extension worker for the government of Zambia. As she taught me how to make nshima, the staple dish of Zambia, she told me, "When it is more important to pay a bank in the

United States than it is to feed our children or provide each community with a school and clinic, we have our priorities out of line."

It is apparent by the growing economic gap between the North and the South that the present-day methods of development are not working. When methods consider the needs of the people and appropriate technology is used, development will come to have a human face. It will become sustainable development. To do this, several elements have to be involved.

Persons, not profits, must be the bottom line and needs, not growth, the top priority. When less than ten percent of the world's population takes part in economic decisions that affect the lives of the other ninety percent, the need to focus on this vast majority when making economic shifts is apparent. When the security of people, and not just nations, is the focus, then monies will be moved from armament to sustainable development, and the needs of the people will be reflected in this move.

Sustainable development, through business and government as partners, can allow people, instead of profits, to be the guiding image. As the marketplace becomes more efficient through privatization, business will need to take on a socially compassionate personality. Decentralization of power, both political and economic, and the involvement of more nongovernmental organizations (NGOs) will empower the poor to be a part of the human face of development.

The role that women play in this new global economy and development is a critical point. This role has gone through at least four different metamorphoses. First, women were viewed as recipients of what men thought they needed. What can we do for them? What is needed to make them better mothers? Men, both in the host country and the donor country, asked these questions. In some cases, this is still the goal and method.

The second came with the dawning of the Decade for Women in 1975, which had the goal of equity for women. Yet for the most part this was a "top down" process. That is, "equal rights" were doled out by the powerful. Women were more involved in development programs, but the decisions were dominated by men. During this time the reason for women being in poverty was seen, by the top men, as resulting from underdevelopment, and not from the lack of control over their own lives. Stressing productivity still did not allow women to set the prices on their own goods.

The third came with the corporate understanding of economic growth and development, profits not people leading the movement for more efficient and effective participation of women in the development arena. The women were aware of what effect it had on them and that this stage was still oppressing women.

The fourth, the empowerment of women, has been the focus since the UN Women's Conference in Nairobi, Kenya, in 1985. It addresses the colonial and neo-colonial mentality of the global economy. Empowered women are self-reliant and have control over their lives—politically, socially, culturally, and economically, allowing women to move forward and claim their place in the global economy.

3

Working Together: Stories from Africa

Because of its vast size and variety of cultures, one cannot generalize about the continent of Africa. Yet there are some historical and economic threads that seem to run throughout Africa. Most of Africa was under colonial rule until the 1950s, when the countries began gaining their independence. England, France, and Portugal were the three principal colonial powers on the "dark continent," as it was often referred to (the mystery of the continent and not the color of the people's skin was the basis for this term), and their rule had both political and economic ramifications. As the colonial powers exploited the natural resources for economic gain, they also exploited the people for political control. It is this legacy of exploitation carried on by the male power structure that continues for the women of Africa.

TIME SAVED—WELL SPENT: ZAMBIA

I met Beauty, the sister of my student Loveness, when I visited her home over a holiday. The sisters lived in a small village of about ten families, fifteen kilometers off the main highway between Lusaka and Livingstone. I waited by the side of the road, at the school gate, until a small lorry came by and gave me a hitch, a ride.

Loveness brought her two younger sisters and her niece, Beauty's oldest child, to greet me and escort me to their home. The two kilometer walk through the tall grass did not seem long. The chattering and singing children surely frightened any snakes that might have wanted to sun themselves on the path.

Coming out of the tunnel of grass into the clearing, a wall of sparkling eyes and shining smiles greeted us. After the customary salutation of one lightly clapping their hands and a deep bow, the children broke into a beautiful song with harmony like only the Zambian people can sing. I felt like I was a queen. President Kaunda could not have had a more regal welcoming.

Loveness's father, the elder clansman, greeted me with a gift wrapped in banana palm leaves. Sitting on a stool carved from a palm tree I carefully opened my gift of a beautiful sculptured face in native wood that had the smoothness and color of my students. It now resides at an honored place in my home.

That night as I lay in the coolness of my sleeping hut, I realized that during the day I had not heard the rhythmic sound of the pounding of maize and the usual singing of the women as they worked. The next morning I asked Beauty about it.

"Come with me to the grinding hut as I grind my mealie-meal and I will tell you about how we got our grinder," she offered. "Back before we had the hand grinder," she explained, "we would gather to pound our maize. We would sing and talk as we pounded. We began to talk about what we could do so we wouldn't have to work so hard. We wanted more time to be with our families. We couldn't afford a tractor, not even one of the small ones that you walk behind. We couldn't lay pipe for the water."

"What about a well? Could a well be dug here near the village?" I asked. The women had to walk two kilometers each way to fetch water. The line of women and girls moving with the grace and flow of a silk scarf, water jug balanced on each head, had been the sight that greeted me as I emerged into the morning mist from my hut.

"The man from the agriculture office says the water is too far down in the ground for us to dig a well. There was no money for a bore hole," Beauty explained as she emptied the plastic pan of mealie-meal into the sack.

"The one thing we all had to do and that took much time was pounding maize. Gloria told us about a grinder her cousin had in her village. We agreed she would find out how much it cost and how they were able to get it. We were beginning to sing new songs about the day we would have a grinder and not have to pound maize again."

"How did you get the money to pay for it? Did you borrow money from the bank?"

As Beauty finished the grinding she explained how they used some of the ideas and ways her cousin Gloria's group did. "No, the bank wouldn't lend us money. The agriculture office wouldn't give us a loan. They said, 'Because you don't own any land we can't loan you any money.' But we said we are determined to get the grinder. As we pounded we talked about ways to earn money. Each woman said she would put in so much. Some women said they would put in K.2 (kwachas), some K.10, one even put in K.20. As we got the money we opened a savings account at the bank. It was then we learned that we had to have papers of organization. We didn't know about papers. We went to your school and asked Mr. Mathea if he would help us write the papers for the organization. He helped us learn how to do it. Some of us wondered why we had to have papers to save some money to buy a grinder. Later we learned why."

Now sitting in the shade and nursing her baby, Beauty continued, "Each woman earned her money in her own way. Some of us raised extra food in our gardens and sold it on the streets of Choma. One woman talked her husband into letting her raise one of his pigs to sell, other women knitted and crocheted things to sell."

"How long did it take you to get the money you needed to buy the grinder?"

"Well, when the bank saw in our organization papers that we would be earning money because we had agreed to pay so much for each bag of mealie-meal that we ground, and that we planned to grind for other women, they agreed to lend us enough to buy it. I think it was about six months. We started at the end of the rainy season and had it by the time we harvested."

"Have you paid off the loan yet?"

"Yes, we paid it off in about a year. Because of the money we made grinding we were able to have all the money that much sooner. This is what we told the man at the bank would happen if he would lend us the money to buy the grinder. Now he is willing to lend us money. We have a good—what you call it—credit, we have good credit now." Beauty's smile told me how happy and proud she was.

"Have you done other things for your village since you women have organized?"

"Now that we don't have to pound maize for four hours a day we've been able to learn things. We've all taken classes from the extension service about food and how to care for our children better. Some women who finished primary school are teaching us how to read and write. Mrs. Tembo at the primary school gave us a book to use. We are now working to build a large building. We will use it for classes in the rainy season. We are working for a clinic. We can come to the building to work together to make things to sell. We make our bricks from the dirt in the anthills."

"It has been hard to find the time to try to make changes here in the village because we still have the many hours of work in the fields and the long walk to carry water but we are making changes," said Beauty.

The grinder symbolizes how Beauty and the other women of the village made and are still making changes. Cooperation not competition, consensus not hierarchical authority, was the model these women used. This model has allowed the women in Zambia to make economic and social changes in their lives. These women in their own way and time changed things and made their lives easier. They learned to use their own resources and the resources of the larger community to make the changes. Their leadership brought about sustainable development locally and nationally, and they taught this woman from the "modern" North how women can empower themselves.

LOCALLY AND INTERNATIONALLY WORKING TOGETHER: GAMBIA

The women of Gambia, like their sisters in Zambia, have also turned their hours and labor of pounding millet into flour into opportunities for both economic and personal growth. As in Zambia, the idea began with the women in the villages wanting to change their lives. Women from fifteen villages, working with the

---

United Nations Development Fund for Women (UNIFEM) and the government of Italy, were able to obtain diesel-powered milling machines. Now the women do in five minutes what had taken them four hours. They must still thresh the grain and remove the husks, but they no longer have to do the hand-blistering work of pounding the millet is done in the mill shed. Now, in addition to more time these women have improved their physical and energy levels also. With less taxing days, the health of the women has improved and so has the health of newborn babies. The lactation level of nursing mothers has increased.

As the news spread throughout Gambia of the mills, other villages sought ways to obtain mills. In 1989 the Gambian Women's Bureau with the help of UNIFEM, took on the project, to acquire a $7 million loan from the World Bank. This was the first women-specific project that the World Bank funded.[1]

A small group of women working together locally tapped into international funds and influenced both the lives of the women in Gambia and the nation's economy. When women empower themselves it is not just their lives that are affected. The circle widens as ripples in a pond when a small stone is tossed into the water. Women are touching women, touching the community, the nation, the world.

WOMEN LEARNING HOW TO ORGANIZE: TANZANIA

As the bus careened around the curve, the chickens in cages lashed to the top of the bus set up a chorus of cackling. The mother beside me was carrying her baby in a cloth sling around her shoulders. Her other little daughter stood between her knees. The breeze that came through the window was hot, but it did relieve the stuffiness of the crowded bus.

Assuming we could not communicate with words, I patted my lap and extended my hands toward the little girl. With a shy glance toward her mother she started to move over. Her mother smiled and said, "Yes, you may."

As I lifted her up I was very aware of how little she weighed. I also could see that the mother's breasts were dry, although the baby she carried was the size of a normal month-old child in the United States. "What is your name?" I asked the little girl.

"She has not learned English yet, but I want to teach her when she is older. Her name is Mary," the mother said.

"You speak English quite well. I thought German was the second language here in Tanzania."

"It is, but I attended a mission school run by missionaries from the United States and England. Though it was not part of the curriculum, we could take special classes in English if we wanted to."

"Do you live in Morogoro?"

"No, I have a sister there. I am on my way to visit her. She is going to take care of my children while I am at the Morogoro Women's Training Center. She will bring the baby over so I can nurse him."

"I am on my way to visit the training center," I said. "This is great! Now you can show me the way there."

"Is not someone collecting you? It is about three kilometers, at the edge of town."

"No, I was not sure when I would arrive and I told them I could walk out."

"How will you carry your things?" she asked.

"On my back. I have not learned to carry things on my head like you women do. I think I am too old to learn how," I explained.

Mary, looking out the window, turned to tell us that we were almost there. By this time my new friend, Elizabeth, and I knew we had mutual concerns. We were concerned about how women in the rural areas could learn how to be better farmers, how to market their goods without going through a middle-person, and what to do about getting the government and agencies to listen to them and learn what their needs were.

Over the next three days, the women at the Training Center helped me to understand how they worked in their villages to increase their crop production and retard soil erosion. Lois told how the Heifer Project[2] had enabled her to become self-supporting. She is now able to send her children, including her girls, to school. She does not have to depend on her husband, who was not always dependable.

I asked Lois to tell me her story.

"My husband works, but I usually do not see any of the money to help with the family. I have two girls and one boy. The boy is the oldest and is usually with his father now, but the girls and I do all the work in the fields and with the livestock. We have three hectares of land and it is close to a stream that runs in the rainy season."

"How do you get water during the dry season?" I asked.

"We used to have to walk about three kilometers to a river, but since I have gotten my goats I could afford to dig a well. There is a woman extension worker in my district. She is the one who told me about the Heifer Project. She helped me get my first goat. I picked goats instead of cows because it is easier to feed them and I can have milk for my children and sell milk. They also provide meat for us. Because of the way the Project works, giving the first female offspring to someone else in the village, there now are several women in my village who have goats. When the Project leader came to our village and taught us about taking care of the goats, we were able to see that we needed to do the same kinds of things for our children. We learned the importance of having a clean place to live, so we got better sanitation for the village. We also learned where to dig the wells. Good nutrition became important to us."

"Elizabeth told me most of the women were heads of households," I said. "Where are the husbands? Are the women widowed, divorced, are the men away at work? Why do the women have to support their families?"

Lois explained, "Most of the women are responsible for support of their families because the menfolk are either not around or they keep the money they make for themselves. I guess you might say it is just the way things are. What makes it worse is that we do not own our land. The land we work belongs to our husbands, fathers, or maybe our sons. Our laws say that women can own land, but our customs are that we do not inherit land. Banks will not lend unless you have land, so we have trouble getting credit. Women have to find their own ways to be self-supporting. There are NGOs, church groups, and UN agents that are helping women more. Some of them are beginning to listen to us but still most decisions are made by men."

"How are you working on your problems?" I asked.

"This Training Center helps us to learn how to organize and to manage money and marketing. We are finding that we can make changes when we work cooperatively. Women make decisions by agreeing, not by someone telling someone else what to do. We know that each of us must help each other if we are to make any gains and have a better life."

The Morogoro Training Center, a church-sponsored center with some funds from the government and a small fee charged for each student, brings together women from around Tanzania to train them in crafts, nutrition and child care, agricultural skills, community organization, marketing, and leadership training. The villages send women like Lois and Elizabeth because they have shown leadership abilities. When the women return to their villages, they work with the women to develop sustainable means of support. By using materials available to them, they develop appropriate technology for meeting their needs. Not all of the women are from rural areas. Some of them come from Dar es Salaam in the rural-urban settlements. Like all large cities, these settlements are filled with women and children who have come to seek employment themselves or have followed their husband. Their needs are much the same, they just have to address them differently.

The women of Africa are women who work cooperatively, with consensus, in community, and with compassion.

4

Women's Work Is Never Ending: Stories from Asia

Asia is even more diverse than Africa and yet we here in the United States often think of the people of Asia as being homogenous. Bangladesh, for example, is a small country that suffers greatly from flooding and other natural disasters. It has very little industry for either domestic consumption or foreign trade. It is not able to be self-sufficient in providing its own food, even though it is principally an agrarian country. Rural women provide most of the labor as well as the management of the farms, but few have title to the land. The land is owned by males in their families. Women are learning ways to empower themselves through cooperative work and credit. The Grameen Bank has been instrumental in helping women to gain some control over their lives.

In India one can see the great disparity between the rich and the poor. There will be families living under palm leaf shelters on the street outside the gate of a wealthy businessman's mansion. There is a democratic form of government and a capitalist economy and strong influences from the Hindu culture. In the rural areas women struggle as do their sisters in the cities for the means to care for their families. Yet, the women are organizing themselves and taking control of their lives.

Reports from the United Nations High Commission for Refugees continue to point out the problems that the women in refugee camps face each day—lack of health care, few opportunities to grow food, poor or no schooling for their children, no way to provide an income, to name just a few. The percentage of women in the camps varies from country to country, but they are always in the majority. The story of the Afghan refugee women in Pakistan, like their refugee sisters in other countries, show how they overcome cultural, economical, and social barriers to make a life for themselves and their children.

The women in the Philippines face different problems than do their sisters in central Asia. The free-trade zones of the TNCs, the debt crisis and foreign military bases impact women in very significant ways. Yet, as their sisters, they still have the worry of feeding and caring for their families and the cultural biases that seem to be universal for all women.

Each country considered here has its own set of circumstances that play out with positive results for the people who glean profits from the operations, and negative results for those who are exploited for the profits.

THE POOR ARE A GOOD CREDIT RISK: BANGLADESH

Who says opportunity doesn't knock twice? While traveling in southern India I met Manisha from Bangladesh, once on a bus from Madras to Kodaikanal and then again when we shared a compartment on a train back to Madras from Madurai. She told me she had worked for the Grameen Bank of Bangladesh, which was started in 1976. She told me how this unique bank had helped the women in Bangladesh. Here is her story.

"In my village most of the people are very poor. Women are not always able to feed their families because there is not enough land to grow food. They didn't have money to buy the food they needed. You know Bangladesh is a very crowded country. There are over 115 million people living on about 55,000 square miles. Our literacy rate is about fifty percent, but much lower for women. Because I had the opportunity to attend a mission school, I can read and write.

"It was back in the late 1970s that I heard of the Grameen Bank. I wrote a letter to the bank asking if someone could come to our village to talk with us. I was able to gather many women in the village when the woman came. After she left, we talked among ourselves about what kinds of things we might do that would help us to make money. Each woman came up with several different ideas. Some provided products to sell and others provided services to be bought. We spent time in looking at what our needs were and how we could meet those needs and provide an income for our families."

"Are loans made to men also, or is the Grameen Bank just for women?" I asked.

"Over seventy percent of the loans are to women. Many men got loans because of the involvement of their wives with the bank."

"From what I have read about the Grameen Bank, it doesn't sound like any bank I know of in the United States. How does the bank reach the women in the rural villages?" I asked.

"Most times it is like in my village. A woman has heard about the bank and asks for a representative to come. In other villages the representatives seek out the village women. I was not able to get a loan because I own a half-hectare (1.235 acres) of land. Our land distribution in Bangladesh is not very equal. Ten percent of the people own forty-nine percent of all the land and only two percent of the land is owned by the poorest ten percent of the people. If you have over one-fourth of a hectare you can't get a loan from the Grameen Bank. But because of my schooling, the bank asked me to be a field representative and work with the people in the village. The women come together in groups of five. Each member has to start out by regularly saving each week."

"What is the level of income in Bangladesh?" I inquired.

"Bangladesh's per capita income of less than Tk.250 ($6.33) per month puts Bangladesh in the lowest .05 percent of the world's countries. Over fifty percent of the landless and assetless people of Bangladesh are women, and of that fifty percent, nineteen percent are women heads of households."

I asked, "How did the women have enough money to save if they were not able to buy the things they needed? It seems to me that it would be very hard to put money into a savings account when your children need food to put in their stomachs."

"It was not the amount that they were saving that was important," said Manisha, "but for them to start saving even one small coin each week told us they would be able to pay back the loans. With this saving pattern set, the women in each group would choose who was to get the first loan. The first woman would have to make several payments on the loan before another woman could borrow. All the members of the group guarantees the loan. This is how the loan is secured.

"There is a leader for each group and that leader meets each week with the bank representative. At these meetings we give out the loan money, collect both savings and payment money, and help the women develop their financial abilities. It is the combination of close supervision, peer group pressure, borrowing only for purposes of generating more income, and the weekly payments, that we have a better than ninety-nine percent repayment among the women."

"This amazes me!" I exclaimed. "I can understand why the traditional banking system wouldn't loan to the women. I know they are as amazed as I am. How did the bank get started? Who put up the money?"

"Mr. Muhammad Yunus, a professor of economics at the University of Chittagong, personally guaranteed bank loans to begin with. Even in the beginning he had ninety-nine percent repayment rate. This was proof enough for him that the poor were a good credit risk. He had stated the bank to give the landless poor an opportunity to break the vicious cycle poverty and have a chance to buy income-earning assets.

"Later, different UN agencies and non-governmental organizations (NGOs) from northern countries put up some capital. You have to realize that the loans are small. The average is Tk.3,000 ($100). We have loaned around Tk.1 billion and have had ninety-seven percent of that paid back in a year and another two percent paid in two years. That is ninety-nine percent paid back in two years. In 1983 we became a registered bank. At that time the government put money into the bank, but seventy-seven percent of the money comes from the borrowers themselves. We have about 300 branches in over 5,000 villages and nearly 250,000 persons involved."

"What are some projects that the women in your village are doing?"

"The largest group is the weavers, not just in my village but in the country. The weavers produce hundreds of thousands of yards of silk saris. There is a ready market for the cloth. Other women raise livestock and vegetables, while others make craft items. We have one person who provides transportation between villages for the elderly with a rickshaw. Another woman provides child care for some cooperative weavers. The women determine the needs of the village and then figure out a way to meet the needs."

With a sense of awe and amazement I asked Manisha, "What would you say was the most important part of the Grameen Bank program?"

Her black eyes sparkled as she spoke, "Giving the women in the villages an opportunity to work together, to improve their lives, and to take control of the economics of their families. We know that women spend their money on the family, while oftentimes the men spend their money on themselves. The women in the villages of Bangladesh who are part of this program are also learning how to get other things for their families and villages. Some of them have begun well-water projects, nutrition and health education, better sanitation, and education for their children as well as for themselves. Now the women smile and know that they can do better for their families."

By 1991, through their requirement that each borrower add one taka per week to their savings account, the Grameen Bank has now accumulated Tk.962 million—sixty-two percent of its outstanding loans. In 1992 the percentage of women members had risen to ninety-two. The success of the Grameen Bank has led to the expansion of that model, not only to many developing countries but also to low-income assetless people in the industrialized North. When given the opportunity to participate in a program that respects and serves their real needs, the poor are good credit risks.

POVERTY DOES NOT STOP THEM: INDIA

As the plane came in for a landing I thought surely we were going to hit some of the shanty town that bordered the runways at Bombay Airport. The huts were so close together I wondered how people walked between them. They seemed to go on for miles. I had been to rural-urban settlements in many major cities of East Africa, yet I had seen nothing like this. I wondered if all of Bombay was what I had seen from the plane.

"I would like to take one of these motorized rickshaws into town instead of a taxi," I told the young man that the church office had sent to meet me at the airport.

"That will take a long time and they are not too safe," he said.

"If we do, I will be able to see more," I replied.

With a disgruntled look he hailed a rickshaw and off we went. I soon began to see that Bombay is a city of great contrasts. We saw people living on the sidewalks with palm leaves woven into shelters, and around the corner were big beautiful homes. The story of Lazarus and the beggar came to mind as we rode through the streets. I also learned that drivers needed only two things to drive in Bombay, a horn and an accelerator pedal. There were times when I understood why the young man said it might not be safe for us to travel this way: if a car didn't hit you, the pollution would make you sick. But I did see Bombay in a way that I never could have from a taxi.

The next morning Lolita asked, "Are you well rested after you trip here? I heard you had an exciting ride in from the airport." We were leaving the mission guest house for a women's center. Lolita, a worker for the Church of South India, was to be my guide for the three days I would be in Bombay. Her ready smile and humorous laughter when she spoke of my rickshaw ride told me I was going to have a delightful time.

"The center we are going to this morning is part of the Christian Medical Association of India," she told me. "They provide the staff and the building. It has many different programs. Today we will visit the clinic and go with one of the women doctors out to make calls in a shanty town. I am taking you at your word—we will be talking with women from different parts of Bombay, as you requested."

When we arrived at the shanty town I realized it was not the one by the airport. There were no planes overhead and here I could smell the sea. While the doctor held her clinic, Lolita and I talked with a social worker.

"What is the biggest problem the women face here?" I asked.

"There is no work for the women, and their children are all malnourished," the social worker explained. "We are assisting them in working cooperatively to generate some income. It is slow but we are gaining. The women have put together a plan to make palm mats that people use in their homes. They know how to weave them, and the mats are light and easy to carry to market. We are helping them learn how to market their goods, how to save some money so they can expand, and how to organize themselves so they can get better services here in the shanty town."

"Who is it you work for? Who pays your salary?" I asked her.

"The city of Bombay employs social workers who work in these kinds of communities, but there is more work than we can do. I am hoping that the women will soon be able to carry on by themselves. Several have leadership qualities, and the women want them to go to school and learn more so they can come back and help them. Two of the women are still living here, but are taking classes at the women's center."

"Where do you get the palm branches to make the mats out of?" I inquired.

"Some of the women spend their time gathering them from the dump where the people who trim trees throw them. The dump is just over that hill. Actually, that hill is an old dump."

"Where do they have to take them to market?" I asked.

"At first we sold them to a man who came around to pick them up, but then we got a bicycle, so now one of the younger women carries them to a marketplace each day. Sometimes when a holiday is coming up she will make two trips a day."

"What do the husbands think about their wives working in public in this way?"

"Many men are not at home," the social worker explained, "and those who are do not work regularly, so they are happy for the women to make some money.

Most of these women are from the untouchable caste. Of course, legally we do not have castes anymore, but the Hindu culture still treats them as outcasts."

The next day at the school I met women who were learning to be leaders in their communities. Most of them were from Bombay. Some of the women work in the factories, and they wanted to learn how to organize so they could have better working conditions. The street vendors were organizing to protect themselves from the middle-person, who usually was a man trying to take advantage of the women. When I asked Lolita how the school was financed, I was happy to learn that about a third of the money came from the students themselves, half from business and professional women in Bombay who want to help their sisters, and a sixth from the city. The center is located in an old mission neighborhood settlement building.

As I boarded the train to leave Bombay for the trip to Madras, I was aware that in all of their poverty and misery these women, both at the center and in the shanty town had a strong spirit of hope. I am not sure I could have so much hope in those conditions.

EMPOWERMENT CAN BE FOUND IN REFUGEE CAMPS: AFGHAN REFUGEES

Although women and children are the majority of the refugees in the world, they usually do not have a say in the running of the camps. Yet, women carry the most responsibility for the family. It is the women who care for the children, obtain fuel and water, and prepare the food. They are also the ones to barter for needed items such as soap, matches, cooking oil, and clothes. The men who organize the camps and relief agencies do the long-term programming. Thus the women are usually treated as nonentities. It is the male refugees who are at the head of the line for training, literacy classes, employment, and income-generating activities. Women are not part of the decision-making process, nor do they have a say in what happens to them.

When the refugees' cultural background restricts the social movement of women, women's experience in the refugee camps can be even more oppressive.

While I was attending the World Council of Churches Conference on Mission and Evangelism, Encuentro 89, in San Antonio, Texas, I met Shanti, who worked at an Afghan refugee camp in Pakistan. She told me that medical services were withheld from women unless a woman doctor could be found. She explained this was part of the Muslim tradition.

"Women have died for lack of treatment," she said. "In many camps where men are in charge of the distribution of the food, sexual harassment of women is common, and girlfriends often receive extra portions.

"In the camp where I work, women realized if they were going to have any control over their lives they must become organized. Men had been making decisions for them. Most of the women were heads of their families yet had no say in what services they would receive. When they found out that the male leadership of the camp had told a relief agency that the women would not be interested in garden plots, the women decided it was time to take control. They went to the relief agent and asked for the garden plots. Then they arranged that the plots be close to where they lived so child care was easier for them. They bartered for a hose to use in watering the plots from the standpipe. With the first seed contributed by the agency, the women soon had fresh food for their families and extra to sell. They made sure that all of the children in the camp were able to have a fresh vegetable each day.

"After getting their garden plots, their next move was to have the right to medical services, despite who the doctor was. They went in pairs for the visits if it was a male doctor. It was not long until the relief agents began to include the women in the decisions about the running of the camp. It was hard for the male leadership to accept women in this role, but the large numbers of women were a force to be reckoned with.

"In this camp the lot of the women improved with the help of the relief agencies. Many women were able to improve their status with literacy classes and by finding new ways to meet the needs of their families. Women working together, sharing in the decisions of how resources are to be used and distributed, has allowed them to have control over their lives and empowered them to move forward."

WOMEN STANDING TOGETHER: THE PHILIPPINES

In 1970 MAKIBAKA: Liberation Movement of New Women (this also means struggle) began to organize the women in the factories. Because of the group's success President Ferdinand Marcos banned MAKIBAKA when he declared martial law in 1972, two years after it was formed. Although the Marcos regime tried to stamp out all resistance, the women became even stronger after the banning of MAKIBAKA. They continued to organize themselves secretly.

As in all countries where the TNCs of the North establish themselves in the free-trade zones the exploitation of women is common even today. The Philippines is no different.

The women in the Philippines as well as in other TNC free-trade zones in Asia, Africa, and Latin America are still in 1990s working under conditions that exploit them. Nena, a worker for Mattel Toy Company, tells of the long hours she worked, from six in the morning to six at night, and the continuous increase in the amount of work to be completed. She has no sick leave or other benefits. If she misses a day she could lose her job. This lack of job security forces her to often go to work when ill. Mattel, like others, wanted to hires women because of the dexterity of their fingers and their more docile nature. Unions are not allowed in the company, leaving the women with no control over their work.[1]

The exploitation of women is also found in the garment industry. A required monthly examination of the breasts and the vagina for virginity is one more harassing ordeal that women workers are put through. The supervisors are looking for young women whom they can control with intimidation and sexual harassment.[2]

GABRIELA: General Assembly Binding Women for Reform, Integrity, Equality, Leadership and Action, named for the woman general in the 1700s, has served as an umbrella for women's groups. Under their guidance the women's movement was very closely tied to the struggle for the liberation of the country. Since the ousting of Marcos in 1986, the women's movement has come more into its own and is able to focus on issues that affect women.[3] GABRIELA reaches out to all women in the cities, squatters camps, rural areas helping women to empower themselves to address the issues of their daily lives.

From the shores of the Pacific to the Mediterranean Sea, the women of Asia reflect a diversity not found in any other continent. The interplay between culture and religion, politics and economics has often held the women back. Now Asian women are using that diversity to empower themselves as they move toward the twenty-first century.

5

Work that Oppresses: Stories from Latin America

Many countries in Latin America are also affected by TNCs and debt crisis as was discussed in the Philippines. Latin American countries have not had the issue of colonial powers to deal with in recent history as have the countries of Africa. Yet there is still a colonial mentality that is part of the economic system in that much of the land and the industry is owned by long-established families that have a collective power in the common goal of economic and political gains. This has led to the widening gap between the rich and the poor. The women again are the ones who experience this gap the most as they try to provide for the care of their families and themselves.

Brazil and Mexico each experienced an economic growth period. Brazil, often referred to as the economic miracle, and Mexico making dollars off its oil. Yet, as we have seen, these gains do not trickle down to the vulnerable at the bottom, the women and children.

Honduras is a small Central American country that was taken over by the United States as it supported and trained the Contras during the Nicaraguan struggle to keep their independence. The U.S. military presence was just one more factor from outside forces that has had a negative impact on the economy of the poor. Honduras also has large TNC plantations producing food for export using the most productive land, leaving little land for local food supply. The lack of land for the campesinas and campesinos in an agrarian culture leads to oppression and poverty.

TNCs OPPRESS WOMEN: BRAZIL

Maria, a Brazilian factory worker, and I were standing in the dinner line as it wound its, way toward the student union at Purdue University. It was a muggy, midwestern summer, a real switch for me from the dry climate of Zambia. I was still adjusting to the culture shock of the United States. Three years is long enough to take on a slower and less harrowing lifestyle.

Maria and I were attending the 1984 Church Women United's global gathering of women. As our conversation led to her work, I asked Maria if she would talk with me about her work in the factory and the women she worked with. After dinner we met out on the lawn and she told me her story.

"My work is on very special machines. I am not sure what we make or what they are used for. Some of them are round and some are long and square like. We women call them *fuba* because we can buy the fuba (corn meal) we need with the money we make. There are only women in my section and we are sealed off from the rest of the plant. We have to wear special clothing and there cannot be any dust in the area," Maria explained.

"The work is routine, but it takes a high degree of concentration and extreme care and attention. We are responsible for carrying out all the different operations in the section: production, photoengraving, etching, and depositing of particles on the round discs. We work with microscopes most of the time. We have to have several months of training, about six months, before we are able to spot all of the defects. What is so troubling is that we are very highly trained and skilled and our supervisors know that we do the best work, yet we are classified as 'unskilled.' There is no chance of promotion to supervisor because they are all men. We women have the lowest wage grade in the plant and that is why the men will not work there. The management does not allow unions. The fear of sexual harassment keeps the women from asking for better working conditions."

"Maria, have you women been able to address any of these problems?" I asked.

"Yes! We have. Though we can't form unions within the factory we do gather in our neighborhoods. Most of us live in the same area. Juanita, one of the women workers, heard the Sisters at her church talk about women working together and making changes. We invited Sister Clara to come to our neighborhood and talk with us. She helped us to realize we could make changes. With her help we organized ourselves into groups of twos. We talked with women in other factories. We found out about wages, working conditions, health hazards, and supervisor abuse. We then wrote a paper about what we had found out. Sister Clara helped us because most of us could not write more than our names. We knew what we wanted to say but she had to write it for us."

"How did you get all of this done with the long hours you work and all of the work you had to do at home?" I asked.

"Well, it took us months because of all the work we had to do, and we didn't have that much support to begin with from our husbands."

"You say, 'to begin with.' Do they support you now?"

"Some of them do. I have been able to show Carlos, my husband, how what I want to do will help the family and our life together. He doesn't like for me to work at all, but he knows that I have to because he can't always find work. He sees how tired I am when I come home and how red my eyes are, so he is now helping me."

"How does Carlos help you?"

"He would not want the other husbands to know that he helps around the house. That would affect his machismo, but he will do the dishes at night and carry in the water from the barrels. Often times he also bathes the children for me."

I asked Maria how she was able to come to this Church Women United gathering here in the United States.

She explained, "First we had to find some way to earn money to help pay my way. The women in the neighborhood made food and sold it and sold other things that they made. Sister Clara was able to get some money from her church. She also knew of some Protestant women in the U.S. who would send us money. We also got money from a UN agency."

"How were you selected to come? Are you the leader of the group?"

"No, we don't have just one leader. Different women do different things. They do whatever they are good at or want to do. They selected me because I had started taking the English classes. We had decided that if we were going to present our concerns to the people who own the company, some of us needed to know some English. I was the one in the group who had finished the most years of schooling. They asked if I would study English with Sister Clara, who is from the United States."

"How did you get off from work to come here? Will you have a job when you return?"

"I left my job to work for the Catholic Church in training women in how to organize themselves not just in the factories but also for better conditions in the communities. I will begin my own training and work when I return. The position with the Catholic Church came about as we worked on gathering the information and presenting our paper of concern to the company. This whole process started about two years ago (1982). Because of my work with the women and one of the women who took the paper to the company I began having more harassment. This has just evolved over the years. I have been studying three nights a week with Sister Clara so my English would improve."

"I wish I was better at speaking a second language. I admire you and all of your courage. We have heard at this meeting about being in solidarity with each other. How can we women here in the United States be in solidarity with you and your sisters in the factories in Brazil?"

"Women involved in social responsibility in investment have been helpful. These women have learned about the conditions that we work under, and have written letters to the companies. Others have boycotted products made by companies that exploit women. They also work to educate other women and men about our working conditions, the environmental and health hazards, and the loss of jobs in your country with plants moving both out of the United States and moving from one state to another within your country. Also we know we are struggling with the same things you are: poor wages, long hours, no health care, sexual harassment. Just knowing that the women in the United States understand that we are sisters in this together gives us courage to continue our struggle."

I have not used Maria's real name or the name of the company because sister-workers would lose their jobs. I can identify that she works for a U.S.-based electronics transnational corporation, where things have not improved since our 1984 conversation. One of the greatest discrepancies in the manufacturing sector is gender discrimination. Not only do women suffer a vertical form of discrimination, by being at the bottom of the job hierarchy, they also suffer horizontal imbalances, with the treatment of men and women being unequal even within the same categories of work.

The metropolitan region of Sao Paulo, where Maria lives, is the industrial heart of Brazil. During the last couple of decades the North has called Brazil "the Economic Miracle," since its Gross National Product (GNP) climbed faster than did any other developing nation's. However, the distribution of wealth in Brazil has not been equitable, as Maria's story tells us. Men are paid more than women. Women are discriminated against. TNCs are there for the profit and not for the people. This has led to debt crisis and even more poverty.

WOMEN DOING MEN'S WORK?: BRAZIL

Not all the inequities in Brazil are found in the manufacturing sector. The agricultural sector also practices discrimination against women. When Acao Democratica Feminina Gaucha (ADFG) was founded in 1964, its focus was on promoting social change in order to give women equal opportunities. Most of the work was in educating women and girls in the urban ghettos. Ten years later in 1974, ADFG turned its sights toward the area of sustainable development and the role women play in agriculture and the environment. A key person in this change of emphasis has been Maria José Guazzelli, an agriculturist specializing in organic farming.

She felt a need to move out of the "Green Revolution"[1] model of production, which relied on expensive chemical fertilizers and pesticides, used only imported hybrid seeds, and cultivated with heavy machinery. These methods gave agribusiness a one-crop basis—soybeans—which was grown for export. For the Green Revolution model to work, there was need for a large acreage of land; this led to the disruption of the family farming and the family structure. It also led to increasing debts for the imported fertilizers, pesticides, seeds, and equipment. It is now known that this type of farming destroys the soil through contamination and erosion. It had no benefits except profits for agribusiness.

In February of 1985, ADFG implemented a project coordinated by women. It combined environmental protection concerns and sustainable development. Located on fifty hectares, in the highlands of southern Brazil near Vacaria, the project has demonstrated how sustainable farming, through terracing and crop rotation, can be viable and improve the conditions of the land—all without the heavy cost incurred through the Green Revolution model.

The Vacaria Project has expanded into the surrounding villages. A woman veterinarian helps to upgrade the livestock through selective breeding and teaches other women how to care for their animals. The methods implemented at the project are taught in the villages across Brazil, and the success of the project is spreading. Students, church extension workers, and international NGOs have sought out the project for training.

Not all has been easy for the women of the Vacaria Project. They face criticism from the large agribusinesses and the government. A project that is in a traditionally male domain, run by two women, brings scorn. ADFG has responded to these critics with irrefutable results, leading the organization to move into the national and international debate on the environment and sustainable development.

"Development will only be socially right and sustainable in the long run if it includes respect for the environment and wise natural resource management as an essential part of decision making," states ADFG organizer Maria José Guazzelli.[2]

Although men are included as associates in ADFG, the board remains all women, and the emphasis on women's issues is central to the organization. The women in the highlands of southern Brazil have found that they—like others—have power when they work together collectively. Like other women working together, the women of ADFG have been able to sustain their families on the land and not be dependent on others. They have regained control over their lives.[3]

THIRD WORLD IN THE THIRD WORLD: MEXICO

The bus was alive with the chatter and singing of students, and the two-hour ride did not seem long. I had joined a sociology class from a university in Cuernavaca on their field trip to the sugar cane fields of Mexico. As we arrived at the camp Professor Cruz said, "You will see the third world in the third world." He was right. This looked very much like villages in the bush of Africa—no drainage for the sewage, one hose from a water truck that came only every other week, children running naked.

I soon became the center of attention as I reached in my pocket and brought out the magic of balloons. I was told there would be more than a hundred children in the camp, so my pockets were bulging. Using the Spanish I was studying, I soon learned from a grandmother that these were only the smallest children. All those over nine years old were out in the fields cutting cane with their sisters and brothers and parents. Only the elderly and the very young were in the camp. I asked the grandmother where she had lived before coming to the cane fields.

"We lived in the mountains to the south. There is not enough work or land for us there so we came here to work. I came along to take care of the children and do the work in the home," she said.

I learned most of the residents were from the mountain areas of the states of Oaxaca and Chiapas and had migrated here to work the cane fields. "We have a nurse, Sister Marjorie, who can tell you about the clinic and school," the grandmother told me.

As I walked among the *ramadas*[4] built out of cane stalks, I heard a voice that had a familiar sound, Spanish with an English accent. In the darkness of the only permanent structure in the camp I could see Sister Marjorie looking into the ear of a small child. When she had finished I asked if I might ask her a few questions. She agreed to take a break from her continuous flow of patients and talk with me.

In her jeans and T-shirt, Sister Marjorie looked more like a college student on a summer outing than a nurse who had given her life to working with the poorest of the poor. As we walked into the shade of a *ramada*, Sister Marjorie asked if I would like a cool drink. Lifting up a wet Mexico blanket, she showed me the welcoming sight of an ice chest. "All I have is an orange and a grape, which will you have?"

Wanting to gulp it down because I was so thirsty, yet sipping it slowly so it would last, I began. "Professor Cruz said these people seem to be the lowest paid workers in Mexico. Is there any hope for them to have better living conditions and higher pay?" I asked.

"The people here are so poor that they have to use most of their energy just to survive. Yet there is hope within these people that I have never found anywhere else. A group of the women did not want to leave everything behind when they came here, so they began meeting in small groups to read and study the Bible as they had done back home. They knew that Jesus did not want them to live as they were living. They also knew that if change was to come it would have to come from them," answered Sister Marjorie.

"I'm surprised that these women can read," I responded, wondering how that had happened. "A grandmother told me that in her village, schooling was only for the boys."

"It is true," Sister Marjorie reassured me, "most of the women cannot read, but there is one who can read a little and she reads and tells the Bible to the others. One day Anita, a young woman from the local Catholic Church, came out to see if the church could do anything to help them with food and clothing. The women told Anita they wanted two things for their children, a nurse and a teacher. That's when I started coming here two days a week. At first the sugar company didn't want the church to interfere at the camp, but the women persisted. Professor Cruz, who brought you here, is a friend of mine, and I asked him if he could send some students here during the summer to teach the children."

"Are you saying that it was the women here in the camp that got the company to provide the teacher and nurse?" I asked in amazement.

"It was the women of the camp through the Basic Christian Community (BCC)"[5] Sister Marjorie explained, "who arranged for me to come, and I helped them get a teacher. They are the ones who insisted that the company allow these services. Anita helped them write the letter and they all signed it. Most of the women know how to write their names. They are now working to get literacy classes for themselves. Along with the clinic, I also work with them on nutrition for their children. The women have also asked the company to provide them with more fresh vegetables. We are still waiting to see what will happen."

"Would you say that the women are the ones who have taken the lead in the improvements in the camp?" I asked.

"Yes, women take the lead in working for the improvement of the welfare of their families and their living conditions. There is one man who is supporting the women, but it is the women who have given the leadership here. The men are only interested in coming home and drinking and playing cards. Some grandfathers, who no longer work in the fields, do help the grandmothers with the garden plots. The problem is there is no water for the gardens and the length of time that the workers are needed in the cane fields for cutting is usually not long enough to grow many kinds of vegetables.

"As the women meet each week for their Bible study, they gain new hope because they see how they are able to apply what they have discussed to their everyday lives. These women have used some very sophisticated analysis to gain the improvement that they have. Back in Ohio, where I come from, my friends just can't believe that these women are capable of this kind of problem solving. I tell them just because they can't read doesn't mean they are dumb. They are very intelligent and by working together they are able to improve their lives."

Sister Marjorie went back to her waiting children, and I joined the others on the bus for a ride to the sugar mill where the cane these workers cut was processed.

A SPECIAL EXAMPLE: HONDURAS

My travels in Central America had not included Honduras, so when Food First in San Francisco invited me to meet Elvia Alvarado I was delighted. I found her most engaging, with a sense of humor that I am sure has carried her a long way in her work with campesinas and campesinos.[6] As Medea Benjamin described in the introduction to the book *Don't Be Afraid, Gringo,*[7] she went to Honduras to write a book about Elvia, and it turned out Elvia wrote the book herself.

Coming from a poor family where her father did not let her sisters go to school and her mother left him because of his abuse, Elvia knew when she was nine years old that the poor would have to be the ones to make changes if changes were to occur. The school in her village only had two grades, but her desire to learn kept her repeating the second grade until she was thirteen.

"My work with the agrarian reform really started when I was trained by the Catholic Church to work with and organize mother's groups," recounted Elvia, as she told her story to those of us gathered in the offices of Food First in San Francisco. She told how most of her work has been with women because the maschimo thinking of the men has hampered her influence with them, but as we listened, we could see that her work with agrarian reform was helping men also. She has organized campesinas, taken their case to the government, and spoken out about the issues affecting the people of Honduras. Imprisonment, torture, and threats to her family are some of the hardships Elvia has endured. Yet, she keeps on going. In her early fifties, a mother of six, grandmother of eleven, Elvia continues to work as an organizer for the National Congress of Rural Workers (CNTC), traveling the back roads of Honduras urging women and men to gain their right to land. Their right to feed their families. Their right to life.

"My faith, both in God and the people of Honduras, is what keeps me going. I know that our economic condition will improve when we have a just political system. Until that happens we have to continue the struggle. We cannot have a free country until the people are free to provide for themselves," Elvia explained. Those of us gathered that day will remember her story, a story of how the women in Honduras have come together to confront the injustices in their lives.

6

Women and Unions: Stories from the United States

WHO MAKES THE PROFITS?

Cameron House, a neighborhood center in the heart of San Francisco's Chinatown, had held a fascination for me since I was a child in Sunday School in rural Missouri. Even my work with friends at the House and San Francisco's Chinatown in my adult life still did not prepare me for Oakland's Chinatown, where dark stairways led to the garment sweatshops. It was a warm sunny November day in 1990 when Young Shin, a Korean lawyer and cofounder of Asian Immigrant Women Advocates (AIWA) took me to see the space where the seamstresses work. I had helped Shin and the staff of AIWA to secure a grant from the church agency where I worked. Many women in the United States work under conditions similar to those found in developing countries. Many of them are immigrants from developing countries.

As we peered through the bars of the door, we could hear the hum of a small fan and the thrummm of the sewing machines, but no voices. The fan did little to circulate the dusty stale air in the room, which had sealed windows. The haze in the air from the lint gave a bluish tone to the dim light coming through the dirt-covered windows. It wasn't long before my nose began to feel dry.

Cloth was piled high on tables, the floor, and window sills. Women were bending over the machines. I could almost feel their backs hurting—it must be hard to sleep at night. Just as we were leaving to go up to the next floor a man yelled at us to "get away and leave my women alone!" For many of these women, the contractors do own them, do have complete control over their work lives. The women are not free to organize unions. If they voice any complaints, they are fired and put on a nonhiring list.

The third floor had two different shops, each sewing expensive women's dresses. Having at one time made all my own clothes and taking two to three days to finish a formal, I was curious: "How many hours does it take to make a lace formal like those hanging on the overhead bar?"

"If it is a special order and only one woman works on it, maybe two hours," a worker told me. She was standing outside the door eating an egg roll for her lunch.

AIWA, a community-based organization of women empowering women, focuses on workers in the electronics, hotel, restaurant, and janitorial industries, as well as the garment industry. Elaine Kim, Pat Lee, and Young Shin, the three cofounders of AIWA, knew the value of women working together for change. They help the women with English and literacy classes, labor rights education, thus gaining more control over their lives as workers and as contributors to the community. Sunday is not a day off for the staff at AIWA, since that is the time they can work with the women and their families. They offer many family-oriented activities.

In May of 1994, AIWA celebrated a decade of challenges. "What a decade it has been!" declared Cai Fen of the Workers Membership Board of AIWA at the celebration. "From a group of Asian immigrant hotel workers getting together to talk about their frustration at work to challenging a giant garment manufacturer to accept corporate responsibility, we have steadfastly worked to empower ourselves and our community."

Fen talked about the many setbacks and victories they had experienced over the past ten years. She stressed that solidarity with others in their community is an important element in their fight for freedom and justice. "In the coming years, many challenges lie ahead of us," Fen stated. "Our community and work place are becoming increasingly hostile places for us immigrants, women, and workers."[1] Fen invited the community to join in the celebration of the strength and spirit of the Asian immigrant women as they reach for their dreams and fight for our rights.

One of those fights began in May of 1992. Twelve Chinese seamstresses from the defunct Lucky Sewing Co. came to Young Shin's office to ask for help. The garment contractor for whom they worked had gone belly up and left them holding an empty bag: $15,000 empty. Along with being angry, they were also desperate. They had worked ten to twelve hours a day, six to seven days a week, for less than $4.25 an hour (minimum wage)—and had not been paid for a month. That meeting with Shin was the beginning of the Garment Workers Justice Campaign, a campaign that has taken on national and international importance.

When it became apparent that the women would not be able to get their money from the contractor, they decided to go to the manufacturer. AIWA determined that Jessica McClintock, Inc., a $145 million company, had been one of Lucky Sewing's exclusive contracts, and thus directed their campaign at Jessica McClintock, Inc.

One of the first things the workers did in the campaign was to visit one of the boutiques in San Francisco that sold Jessica McClintock fashion dresses. What the women saw there made them even angrier: they had received $5 to make a dress which sold for $175!

The Public Media Center in San Francisco helped them launch a detailed and aggressive public relations operation. Full-page ads in the *New York Times* got the word about the campaign out across the country. That fall, on the day after Thanksgiving—the biggest shopping day of the year—workers in ten cities, including New York, Chicago, and Los Angeles rallied in support of the campaign.

Picketing the Sutter Street boutiques and up-scale department stores of San Francisco became the strategy. "Jessica, Jessica, stitch by stitch; sweatshop labor made you rich," the women chanted while carrying their hand-lettered placards and lifting above the bustling shoppers some Jessica McClintock lace dresses, donated by an activist woman.

On the following May 1, 1993, Labor Day for most of the world, AIWA held a community hearing in Oakland: "Immigrant Women Speak Out On Garment Industry Abuse." Both local and state officials and their aids listened to testimony from people involved as well as a panel of expert witnesses. It was there that Fu Lee, one of the twelve seamstresses who had sought out the help of AIWA, told her story.

Fu Lee is a forty-one-year-old married woman with a nine-year-old daughter who has been living in Oakland Chinatown since leaving Hong Kong twelve years ago in 1981.

She worked as a seamstress at Lucky Sewing Co. for two years, and before there she worked as a seamstress at other similar sweatshops. "We all worked long hours, ten to twelve hours a day and six to seven days a week," Fu Lee said. "We were paid by the piece, which sometimes amounted to below the minimum wage. Overtime pay was unheard of. You may think sewing is an easy job. But it requires a lot of skill. For fancy dresses, with laces, tiny buttons, and tricky fabric patterns, you really have to concentrate so you don't make any mistakes. My wage was never enough money for our family to live on. We always worried about our daughter getting sick because we had no health insurance."

She told about the eye strain because of poor lighting, how her throat hurt because of the chemical fumes from the fabric dye—even when she would wear a surgical mask so she would not have to breathe in all the accumlated dust.

"Our boss was like a dictator," she explained. "He was always pushing us to work faster. There was a sign in the shop which said, 'No loud talking. You cannot go to the bathroom.'"

Fu Lee told of the anger and frustration the twelve Chinese seamstresses felt. She told how her boss was paid only $10 for a $175 dress and how the seamstresses recived less than $5. She explained how Jessica McClintock had terminated its contract with her employer after ten years of exclusive dealings.

"We felt that since Jessica McClintock made the most profit from the dresses we sewed, she should pay us for our work when our boss can't," Fu Lee said. "So we asked Jessica McClintock, Inc. to pay us our back wages."[2]

The seamstresses wore masks when they picketed because they were afraid of being blacklisted in the garment industry; if they were called troublemakers, they would have a difficult time finding a job. Immigrant women with their limited

English are caught in these dead-end jobs. But instead of listening to their demands, Jessica McClintock called the public rallies and picketing "a blatant shakedown and intimidation."

This is not a unique story. San Francisco Bay's garment industry is the third largest in this country. It employs over 25,000 garment workers, eighty percent of whom are women, most of them immigrants. For over a century, immigrant women have been the backbone of America's garment industry. They make up about seventy-seven percent of the 800,000 garment workers in the United States. Only about twenty-five percent of these workers belong to unions. Manufacturers use immigrant women's labor because it's cheap and little is known about the awful working conditions.

Economic issues often cannot all be settled in the corporate board room or on picket lines. The last two governors of California, George Deukmejian and Pete Wilson, have vetoed proposed state legislation to make garment manufacturers and contractors jointly liable for working conditions and wage scales. But one assemblywoman is not willing to give up. Hilda L. Solis, from El Monte in Southern California, carried Assembly Bill 3046 in 1994. There was little hope that Wilson had changed his mind, but the women in this campaign have the tenacity of a bull dog. They will not give up. While campaigning for Proposition 187, Governor Pete Wilson vetoed Assemblywoman's Solis bill, blaming the conditions of the women on the "abysmal failure of the federal government to prevent massive illegal immigration into California," thus scapegoating immigrant workers, not manufacturers, for sweatshop wages and working conditions.

The San Francisco Bay Area is not the only place where the garment industry runs sweatshops. New York has more than 4,000 employing 50,000 workers for an average of 12.5 workers per shop. Los Angeles also has a large garment industry. The success of this campaign will have a ripple effect to these other cities.

The contractors who run the sweatshops are in a highly competitive business. Many times they have to bid so low to get the contract that they are not able to pay minimum wage. The contractors are often people who have been seamstresses and moved "up" in the business.

Duke Tu, a Vietnamese immigrant contractor, wanted some of the other contractors to appear with him at the May 1 hearing in Oakland, but they were afraid to speak out openly. Tu told of the control the manufacturers have on setting the price and the fierce competition between contractors. Although fashion manufacturers have been doing well during the severe recession in California since the early 1990s, Oakland has lost over two-thirds of its contractors' shops.[3]

Those in the garment industry are aware of how production is being moved out of the country. From the *maquiladoras*[4] that stretch the length of the Mexico-U.S. border, the free-trade zones in the Pacific Rim countries, Latin American countries, and southern Asia, the garment industry has become a global issue. The pay of garment workers in Mexico is $4.50 a day. In Guatemala, where Koret moved its production after closing a union shop in San Francisco, the workers make $2.00 a day, and in El Salvador the pay is even less.[5] Trade agreements like the North American Free Trade Agreement (NAFTA) and the General Agreements of Tariffs and Trade (GATT) treaty will only contribute to the problem. Manufacturers will keep production of their garments in the United States only if they can keep costs down. Thus low wages, unsafe working conditions, and longer hours will continue in sweatshops because of the lack of controls in the industry.

To show their solidarity with AIWA and the garment workers, the following unions joined the picketing on July 30, 1994: Amalgamated Transit Union Local 155, Hotel Employees and Restaurant Employees Local 2, Service Employees International Local 250, Teamsters Local 856, and the San Francisco Central Labor Council. On August 15, 1994, Jessica McClintock, Inc., filed three complaints against AIWA and the labor unions with the National Labor Relations Board (NLRB).

Immigrant seamstresses and their supporters expressed disappointment at the restrictions placed on their free speech rights in protesting garment manufacturer Jessica McClintock. On August 25, ten days after filing with the NLRB, San Francisco Superior Court Judge Stuart R. Pollack granted a preliminary injunction that curbed the picketing efforts of the garment workers and their supporters. The protesters had to march at least six feet away from the entrance of McClintock's boutique; only one person from each side of the dispute could leaflet inside the six-foot prohibited zone; and only two people could march in front of McClintock's residence, with up to five additional people on the entire block. McClintock's complaints were dismissed the first of December, 1994.

As one immigrant woman said at a Union Square Rally in San Francisco, November 19, 1994, "We will continue with this campaign until we win our demands! We say this because this campaign is not just for us but for every immigrant woman who suffers in silence. We want McClintock to show corporate responsibility to the immigrant women workers who made her rich. We want her to have the respect to sit down with us and work out a fair and just solution to this problem."

What part do the women in the United States play in the exploitation of women in the garment industry? How can U.S. women support their immigrant sisters here in our country and in the *maquiladoras* of the free-trade zones? Although Jessica McClintock is a shining example for the modern-day business woman, she has built a million-dollar business by using cheap labor to increase her profits. But how is this example different from other business examples? What part does corporate responsibility play in making certain that economic justice is there for all, workers and business-persons alike? These are questions that will need to be answered as solutions to inequities are sought in the global economic order.

"This is more than a labor issue," says Young Shin of AIWA. "Fundamentally, it's a human-rights issue. Unless someone speaks up, I'm afraid it's going to get worse."

"A responsibility for justice is not just for ourselves," declares Cecilia Rodriguez, a founder of *La Mujer Obrera* (The Woman Worker), "but a responsibility to others around the world because they are our brothers and sisters, the source of our cultures and history. We must work in organizations which will fight for better rights.

"The most important legacy we must pass on to our children, to future generations is a 'life with dignity.' To be oppressed is to die a thousand deaths every day. A life with dignity does not come with money, or fame, or power which leaves one empty and greedy for more, but the knowledge that we have lived our lives fighting to bring justice and peace to the world."

Rodriguez explained the role that immigrants have played in the history of labor in the United States in her speech in June 1994 at the Tenth Anniversary of AIWA. "The struggle in America is very important. In its history it has been immigrants who have changed conditions here, it was immigrants in the 1800s who established an eight-hour day, immigrants who fought for the right to organize, for the right to have Social Security, for the right to have the few labor laws which protect workers."[6]

Across the country in New York City, immigrant women are addressing the same issues. The Chinese Staff and Workers' Association (CSWA) held a conference in July 1994 on Workers' Centers and the New Labor Movement: Our Model and Our Vision. The Women's Empowerment Project of CSWA was a part of this conference, as was Young Shin of AIWA and Maria del Carmen of *La Mujer Obrera* of El Paso, Texas.

Participants at this conference learned that the U.S. labor force is being transformed into a contingency work force. One of the major changes is the move to part-time, temporary, and contract jobs. This contingency work is one-third of the U.S. work force and makes up over half of the new employment created each year. Although the percentage of men has grown faster due to the recession layoffs, women still make up well over fifty percent of this work force.[7]

The issues that this restructuring brings up are not being addressed by most union leadership. The model that women have been developing over the last decade, on the other hand, is one that merits study. They have established multitrade centers that work with women from many different industries. They focus on the workers and their families and the community. These centers are organized from the bottom up—grassroots and participatory. They work on all issues that affect the workers—political, economic, and social. By providing both a place to meet and resources for the development of leadership within oppressed groups, this is a model that minority groups, especially women within minority groups can benefit from. This model is interested in justice, not just jobs.

Wing Lam, executive director of CSWA, sums it up this way in the Summer 1994 issue of CSWA News, "Underlying the vision of this new labor movement is an understanding that economic, social, and political justice can only become a reality when working people organize to take power into their own hands. This means organizing in our communities to develop new social relations that challenge the priority of profits over people's needs."

On March 18, 1996, Labor Secretary Robert B. Reich announced an agreement between Jessica McClintock, Inc. and Asian Immigrant Women Advocates bringing to a close a three-year battle over wages and contracts between the two organizations. The agreement would not let AIWA discuss how the agreement was reached. "'This agreement signifies an important milestone in efforts to establish cooperative relationships among all levels of the industry,' said Reich. 'I commend both parties for reaching this agreement.' The agreement calls for cooperative efforts by both parties to insure workers' rights as well as to promote awareness of fair labor practices." These efforts will include various educational components, services and materials in both English and Cantonese, and monitoring of wages and conditions. [8]

PART II

POLITICS AND WOMEN
DO MIX

7

Voting Is Not Enough

Women have a "herstory" of political involvement in the United States. Abigail Adams, a leader for women during the Revolutionary period in the United States, said to her husband, "If particular care and attention is not paid to the ladies we are determined to foment a rebellion, and will not hold ourselves bound by any laws in which we have no voice or representation."[1] Women did win the right to vote in 1920, but in the last three-and-a-half decades there has been a reemerging of the women's story.

The herstory of women's involvement in the political process has had its peaks and valleys. "The sex stereotypes and legal restrictions that so severely hampered women's activities in the nineteenth century were relatively weak in the eighteenth. Consequently women participated in the social, economic, political, and military activities of the day in ways that would be thought highly improper, if not impossible, for women a generation later."[2]

Middle-class women in the 1950s had heard of suffragists winning the right to vote, though I dare say many could not have told you that it was the Nineteenth Amendment to the Constitution, ratified in August 1920, that gave them that right. Once women gained the right to vote, their goal had been met, most of them put away their placards and sashes and stayed home. With the Roaring Twenties, the Great Depression of the thirties, and the war of the early forties most women became indifferent to the women's movement. The Irish playwright, George Bernard Shaw, a feminist, said in 1927, "People sometimes wonder what is the secret of the extra-ordinary knowledge of women which I show in my plays. I have always assumed that a woman is a person exactly like myself, and that is how the trick is done."[3] He helped to keep the small flame alight during those indifferent times.

Women left the home to do their part during World War II in the defense factories, but when the "boys came marching home," they put away their riveters and hair snoods and took up their dust mops and aprons. During the late forties and the fifties, young women were indoctrinated in how to be a "good housewife." Their identity was found in what followed the "Mrs." part of their name. In the 1960s, all that changed. Many women reading Betty Friedan's *The Feminine Mystique* felt they were reading their own biography. They began to question the feelings they were having about themselves. Some questioned why they had gone to college. If they had gone to work from high school, they questioned their salaries. The house, kids, and hubby were just not fulfilling life for them.

The winds of change forced open the door of indifference in the 1960s, and the women's movement came into its own again with the establishment of Friedan's National Organization for Women (NOW). The Equal Rights Amendment (ERA) gained new momentum with its passage in Congress in 1972. The 1970s saw many different bills passed: Equal Credit Opportunity Act, Pregnancy Disability Act, Title IX of the Education Amendment, Fair Housing Act, and the Tax Reform Act of 1976 that allowed for some child-care deductions. These were all follow-ups to the bills and Executive Orders in the 1960s that dealt with sex discrimination.

There have been more peaks and valleys over the last two decades. The growth of the conservative Right in the eighties caused the defeat of the ERA. The landmark Supreme Court decision of *Roe vs. Wade* and the pro-choice movement of the seventies have felt the impact of the antiabortion movement in the eighties and nineties. Yet the followers of Phyllis Schafly, head of the Eagle Forum and one of the foremost conservative women leaders, would have us believing that women have gained equal rights.

These "gains" were questioned by Susan Faludi in her book *Backlash*. Faludi asks the "Why?" questions about the number of poor women with poor housing, no health care, and no pensions. She asks about the seventy percent of working women making less than $20,000 a year. The disparity in pay and jobs between educated men and women is questioned. She highlights the role of women in politics, showing they are far from equal. There is a continuing backlash, propagandized through the media, by the religious Right, and political conservatives.

The Clarence Thomas hearing jolted many women out of their apathy. "They just don't understand," became a resounding cry. Naomi Wolf in *Fire with Fire* calls the Anita Hill testimony exposing Thomas's alleged sexual harassment the "genderquake."[4] The threat of losing abortion rights, the legitimizing of sexual harassment charges, the increasing awareness of both physically and sexually abusive behavior to women and children has blown the door open again in the early 1990s. The question is how long will the door stay open, or will frustration and apathy slam it shut again.

We need to recognize that the dominant masculine—patriarchal—power structure has been used to put women as well as men in positions of leadership. (Though many women see this as tokenism.) When I use the terms "men" or "women power" this is another way of saying masculine or feminine power—patriarchal or egalitarian power. Naomi Wolf assures women of their political power if they are willing to work together. She also makes it clear that there are men in this fem-nine—egalitarian—movement for power. "The women's movement had twenty years to critique traditional femininity, and it was clear from early on that women stood to gain far more than they had to lose. Men have only begun to critique traditional masculinity, and the promised rewards for doing so are still faint, while the treasures to be lost and the punishment threatened are far more vivid and immediate."[5]

We all know that anyone with power is not going to give it up freely, be it man, woman, or nation. Yet there are some who are willing to share power. Wolf speaks of these people: "Under this pressure, the world of men is dividing into egalitarians and partriarchalists—those men who are trying to learn the language and customs of the newly emerging world, and those who are determined to keep that new order from taking root. . . . The civil war of gender does not involve 'men against women' on two distinct sides. The patriarchalists' worldview, shared by women as well as men, is battling the emerging egalitarian worldview, which is also shared by people of both sexes."[6]

WOMEN'S MOVEMENT IS GLOBAL

"Feminism has no particular ethnic identity,"[7] states Kumari Jayawardena, a Sri Lankan feminist writer. There are no boundaries in the women's movement. It is global.

While I was living in Zambia men often said to me, "This whole business of women's liberation was imported from the United States." Yet as women look back in their herstory they find that there have been feminists laying the foundation for the contemporary women's movement for decades. Kumari Jayawardena in her book *Feminism and Nationalism in the Third World* states, "Many people in the Third World are not aware that their countries have a history of active feminism, or of early movements for women's emancipation, that were supported both by women and men reformers."[8] She goes on to say that she believes that the people who are dismissing feminism as a foreign import are using that idea to keep women in a subordinate position. She encourages women to come together at all levels, gaining strength to free themselves from exploitation, oppression, and patriarchal structures.

Jayawardena also expresses her understanding of why there is a feminist movement. "It is in the context of the resistance to imperialism and various forms of foreign domination on the one hand, and to feudal monarchies, exploitative local rulers, and traditional patriarchal and religious structures on the other, that we should consider the democratic movement for women's rights and the feminist struggles that emerged in Asia."[9]

It is not just in Asia where you hear women declaring their frustration with their role. In Zambia, Joyce—the wife of one of the professors at the college where I taught—told me, "If the men in this country think we women are going to sit still and let them continue to control our lives they are mistaken. We have ERA, equal rights, written into our constitution but the women in the United States have more rights than we Zambian women have. We are mad, plenty mad, and we are going to draft some laws that the National Assembly will have to take heed of." We were on the train headed for Lusaka, the capital. She was a delegate from her district to a called meeting of the Women of UNP (United National Party).

PEACE *SHALOM*: WOMEN IN THE FOREFRONT

Recognizing the need to empower themselves in their struggle for the liberation of their country and to liberate themselves from oppressive culture, Filipino women had the impudence to form GABRIELA (General Assembly Binding Women For Reforms, Integrity, Equality, Leadership, and Action) on April 28, 1984. It began with forty-two affiliated organizations from all sectors. Taking the name of General Gabriela Silang the first Filipino women general, GABRIELA, took a lead in the liberation movement and supported Corazon Aquino for president.

In Latin America, mothers have been in the forefront in the peace movement. The Mothers of the Plaza de Mayo in Argentina in nonviolent protest demanded to know the whereabouts of their sons, husbands, and daughters. In their black dresses and white head scarfs they gathered to protest in the heart of Buenos Aires. The mothers of Guatemala formed the *Grupo de Apoyo Muturo* (Mutual Assistance Group). In El Salvador they called themselves the *Co-Madres* (Committees of Mothers of the Disappeared). In each group the mothers, sisters, and wives have led the struggle against imperialism and the destruction of their society. Many have been imprisoned, raped, tortured, and killed. The solidarity of the women and their courage and faith have given them the strength to lead and fight in nonviolent ways for human rights and dignity.

WHO MAKES PUBLIC POLICY AND HOW?

The role of women in forming public policy is still limited. There have been notable women leaders in many developing countries: Benazir Bhutto, president of Pakistan; Golda Meir, prime minister of Israel; Indira Gandhi, prime minister of India; Corazon Aquino, president of the Philippines; Violeta Barrios de Chamorro, president of Nicaragua; Nabeela al-Mulia, ambassador to Zimbabwe for Kuwait; Anna Popowiez, minister of women and family affairs, Poland; veiled women from the capital district of Muscat of Oman who took seats in the Majlis al-shura Council in 1994. Yet the ability of these women leaders to make a sustained change in women's participation in policy formation has been minimal. Women at the grassroots level are now gaining a voice in some policy making that affects their lives. Although some of those voices are moving up to higher levels of government, limitations remain.

The elements that restrict women's involvement in policy-making at the national level are similar to those that are found at the international level. Using Hans Morganthau's six principles of political realism from his book *Politics Among Nations*, J. Ann Tickner looks at his masculine world view and compares it with feminist theory. Tickner summarizes Morganthau's principles as follows:

1. Politics, like society in general, is governed by objective laws that
    have their roots in human nature, which is unchanging: therefore
    it is possible to develop a rational theory that reflects these objective
    laws.

2. The main signpost of political realism is the concept of interest defined
    in terms of power which infuses rational order into the subject matter
    of politics, and thus makes the theoretical understanding of politics
    possible. Political realism stresses the rational, objective and
    unemotional.

3. Realism assumes that interest defined as power is an objective category
    which is universally valid but not with a meaning that is fixed once
    and for all. Power is the control of man over man.

4. Political realism is aware of the moral significance of political action.
    It is also aware of tension between the moral command and the
    requirements of successful political action.

5. Political realism refuses to identify the moral aspirations of a particular
    nation with the moral laws that govern the universe. It is the concept
    of interest defined in terms of power that saves us from moral excess
    and political folly.

6. The political realist maintains the autonomy of the political sphere;
    he asks 'How does this policy affect the power of the nation?' Political
    realism is based on a pluralistic conception of human nature. A man
    who was nothing but 'political man' would be a beast, for he would
    be completely lacking in moral restraints. But, in order to develop
    an autonomous theory of political behavior, 'political man' must
    be abstracted from other aspects of human nature.[10]

Tickner believes there are multiple realities. These realities reflect a more
inclusive way of viewing policy formation. She writes, "A truly realistic picture
of international politics must recognize elements of cooperation as well as conflict,
morality as well as *realpolitik*, and the strivings for justice as well as order."[11]
It is with these multiple realities that Tickner formulates her own six principles,
from a feminist perspective.

1. A feminist perspective believes that objectivity, . . . is associated
    with masculinity. Therefore, supposedly 'objective' laws of human
    nature are based on a partial, masculine view of human nature. Human
    nature is both masculine and feminine; it contains elements of social
    reproduction and development as well as political domination.
    Dynamic objectivity offers us a more connected view of objectivity
    with less potential for domination.

2. A feminist perspective believes that the national interest is multidimensional and contextually contingent. Therefore, it cannot be defined solely in terms of power. In the contemporary world the national interest demands cooperative rather than zero sum solutions to a set of interdependent global problems which include nuclear war, economic well-being and environmental degradation.

3. Power cannot be infused with meaning that is universally valid. Power as domination and control privileges masculinity and ignores the possibility of collective empowerment, another aspect of power often associated with femininity.

4. A feminist perspective rejects the possibility of separating moral command from political action. . . . The realist agenda for maximizing order through power and control give priority to the moral command of order over those of justice and the satisfaction of basic needs necessary to ensure social reproduction.

5. While recognizing that the moral aspirations of particular nations cannot be equated with universal moral principles, a feminist perspective seeks to find common moral elements in human aspirations which could become the basis for de-escalating international conflict and building international community.

6. A feminist perspective denies the autonomy of the political, since autonomy is associated with masculinity in Western culture, disciplinary efforts to construct a world view which does not rest on a pluralistic conception of human nature are partial and masculine. Building boundaries around a narrowly defined political realm defines political in a way that excludes the concerns and contributions of women.[12]

The role women play at any level of policy formation, be it in the family or international arena, will have to deal with the issues that Tickner has raised. Although women are frequently cast in the role of leadership on social and welfare issues, it is a leadership that follows the policies determined by men. These policies often do not address the needs of women and the families for whom they are responsible. Women have shown they are interested in formulating policies that effect change at the root causes of their oppression and exploitation, and they are not interested in carrying out "band-aid" measurers and catch-up procedures.

IDEOLOGIES: POSITIVE AND NEGATIVE

The parts that ideology plays are crucial in understanding the role of women in policy formation. Ideologies can be both positive and negative. This is determined by the cultural and social-political levels of the people involved. If the people are looking for tools for sociopolitical analysis or construction, or to develop conscientization[13] then the ideology will have a positive interpretation. If it is viewed as a tool for deception, exploitation, oppression, and domination, than it is a negative tool. As suggested by Tickner, the masculine and feminist viewpoints can be quite different; thus the support of a particular ideology will also have this determining factor. "Wrestling with ideologies is inevitable, and inasmuch as ideologies leave no space untouched in both the human self and in the world, that wrestling has become a very crucial one."[14]

Among the many problems women face when a feminist perspective is not part of the policy making is in claiming ideologies that appear to be democratic but in fact are totalitarian. At a 1988 gathering of Christian leaders for a Consultation on Ideologies the question was asked, "Is it not really the case that ideologies of power are usually authoritarian to say the least and that the content of their political rhetoric is democratic whereas their actual political praxis is totalitarian?"[15]

The ideologies of war and peace are prime examples of the roles that men and women play. The peace movement, not just in the United States but around the world, is heavily populated by women. It is the women who suffer the most from modern-day war. Men no longer go out to a "battlefield" and fight a duel between two nation-states. War today encompasses all of creation; women, children, ecosystem, and men. Men are involved in the peace movement, but it is the women who are carrying the dove high. It is men who are in the majority when it comes to planning and carrying out wars. It is women's diplomacy—with a focus on knowing and understanding those who are from a different background, and not calling them the "evil empire," the enemy; searching for common ground and concerns, respecting differences and allowing for various approaches to a problem; working together in agreed areas—that will lead to a true peace, *shalom*, and not just the absence of war.

Two of the worlds leading ideologies, capitalism and socialism, offer few advantages to the disempowered women of the developing countries. Capitalism is seen as self-seeking and greedy, with the strong preying on the weak. The structure of capitalism controls the flow of money/power and has caused exploitation and domination that has led to the debt crisis. Following the premise of "might makes right," capitalism has encouraged the arms build-up and supported repressive governments that create a "secure" environment in which to do business and make investments. The preservation of the ecosystem is not one of capitalism's top priorities; when United States, Mexico, and Canada were discussing trade negotiations the issue of environment was not even taken up. The Canadian Minister of International Trade told the House of Commons that the North American Free Trade Agreement (NAFTA) was a commercial agreement and, therefore, environment issues were not on the table.[16]

This is not to say socialism outshines capitalism. The women in the developing countries can see its ugly and inhuman past. They are aware that it does not guarantee genuine participation of all the people in the political process. Totalitarian rule is as likely in a socialist ideology as in a capitalist. In many developing countries the women are developing their own ideology that is a mixture that addresses their needs. There is a market economy with the street vendors and cottage industries, but they also know that they have to work together cooperatively for the community if the individual is to gain. People, not profits, is the bottom line. As women gain in leadership skills and community development, we see them taking on the responsibility of policy formation.

CONCLUSION

There are many ways that women have made gains as they have joined together in each country and as the women's movement has grown. "Mutual problem-solving, sharing of information, division of labor, efforts at creating coalition and unity, mobilization and recruitment of activists, and the gaining of positive access of media and government—all of which were to be built upon in future political efforts—emerged," say Joyce Gelb and Marian Lief Palley in their book *Women and Public Policies*.[17] Although they were referring to the women's movement in the United States, women the world over are finding the same benefits emerging in their own women's movement.

The stories that follow illustrate how women are becoming more involved in policy formation and decision making—how they develop their own ideologies as they work for peace, *shalom,* and justice.

8

Women of Courage: Stories from Africa

THE PEN MIGHTIER THAN THE SWORD: EGYPT

The herstory of Egypt lists many women who have been political leaders. The future herstory will add the name Nawal el Saadawi, a medical doctor, writer, and a feminist activist. She does not belong to any political party, nor has she ever taken up a gun or sword to wage a battle against injustices. She uses something mightier than a sword—her pen.

Saadawi's predecessors in the 1919 revolution focused on the national issue of independence from Britain. From that upheaval grew the Egyptian Federation of Women (a.k.a. Egyptian Feminist Union), under the leadership of Hoda Shaarawi. Though the Federation led the way in the early days of the suffrage movement, after the death in 1947 of Hoda Shaarawi it lost much of its influence as in-house feuding led to the forming of a new organization called Daughter of the Nile in 1949. "Using a much more confrontational strategy than the Feminist Union did, they engaged in a series of protests, including storming Parliament in 1951 to protest the exclusion of women from membership."[1]

The agenda of both organizations was women's rights but, as we have seen in many other countries, once women have gained the right to vote, their energy takes a different direction toward more charitable and social-welfare issues. Another component that often leads to diminished activism on women's rights is the make-up of the movement. When leadership of the movement is from the upper and middle classes and the poor and working class are not part of policy formation, the focus is often on issues unrelated to social justice—on the symptoms rather than root causes.

The consciousness of the ebb and flow of the women's movement has returned to Egypt from the pen of Saadawi. After her imprisonment in 1981 when Anwar el Sadat was president, Saadawi reflected, "An obvious conclusion is that the

conceptions and aims of women's liberation must perforce be a serious threat to
the very roots of patriarchal society—mainly because they do *not* recognize separation
among political, social, economic, cultural, psychological, and sexual oppression."[2]

Believing that women are excluded from the main decision-making
arenas—religion, philosophy, politics, and economics—Saadawi stresses that women
must develop their own power. She called this message forward with the forming
of the Arab Women's Solidarity Association, (a.k.a. Association of Solidarity
Between Women (ASBW)). This pan-Arab association for women's rights has
an international flavor, although Saadawi firmly believes that any movement has
to begin with the individual woman. Change comes first in the individual, then
in the home, and on out to the community. Although she does not belong to a
political party, she created quite a stir when she advocated that women form their
own party. She writes, "When I wrote in Cairo that women should start a political
party, everybody was angry, even the Marxists."[3]

It is with this political power on the national level that Saadawi sees a movement
toward international influence. The relationship between the control of global
economics and the power of the transnationals (TNC) has its heritage in the
patriarchal relationship to imperialism and capitalism. Until women begin to build
their own power base in solidarity with women in other countries, they will continue
to exist under patriarchal domination. With the fervor of a champion, Saadawi
asserts, "We have to continue to make the link between this international oppression
and the exploitation and the oppression of women."[4]

The struggle goes on: "If I want to unveil the Arab mind and fight for change,
I must keep on. As long as I am not satisfied I will write. I'm ready to die if
someone stops me from expressing myself," she says.[5] The Arab Women's Solidarity
Association was terminated by the Egyptian government in August of 1991 "on
the pretext that it violated a law forbidding such groups to discuss politics."[6]
The ebb has come again, and the flow of the women's movement is being countered
by a strong political and religious fundamentalist movement. Despite the ideology
of the time, Saadawi encourages women; "We must claim those things that are
positive, and discard without hesitation those things that are negative."[7]

Saadawi, an example for women around the globe, gives us a model of courage
and power. She inspires us to use our talents and stand strong in solidarity with
our sisters.

A LEGACY NOT TO BE FORGOTTEN: SOUTH AFRICA

The role that women played in bringing apartheid to an end is a legacy and
cannot be forgotten. We have much to learn from these women of valor. As in
most struggles, there are the great leaders, and there are legions of the faithful
followers. That is the story of the women who fought apartheid. It was the African
women that carried the load, but support came from colored, Indian, and white
women, too. There were women in South Africa and women in exile, women
in hiding and women in prison, women banned and women who traveled freely,

and the women in the churches whose faith carried them when all else seemed to fall away. I met one of these exiled women while in Zambia, where the African National Congress (ANC)[8] had its exile headquarters.

Women in Exile

The golden miniature Christmas tree blossoms of the mango tree helped to assure us that there might be a good harvest. The spreading guava trees and the mango trees gave us the shade we needed to have a cool place to sit and talk. My friend Edna brought a South African woman, Zellda, for a visit. I never knew Zellda's real name. She had been a leader with her husband in the African National Congress (ANC) in South Africa.

When Zellda's husband and his brothers were taken from her home one night by armed men, Zellda, from her hiding place under the floor, heard the men say, "We will get the 'bitch' tomorrow." She knew she had to take her children and flee. She lives in Livingstone, Zambia, and is still working for the ANC. She had come to my home with one of my YWCA friends. This is her story.

"The women in South Africa carry a double-triple burden. Double in that we are oppressed because we are women and African. Triple in that we have to produce, reproduce, and service the community. I sometimes wonder why women even bother to get married with all the work we have to do. My husband was home some of the time, but he never contributed much for rent or food or care of the children. I was fortunate that my mother lived with me when my children were small and she was able to care for them while I worked and after I got involved with ANC."

"How did you get involved in ANC? Was it through your husband?"

"No, it was the other way around. I came home one night from a meeting and he was angry with me and started to accuse me of being out with a man. I told him why didn't he come with me the next night and see where I have been and what we are doing. That was when my mother spoke up and told him to either go or shut up. Mother was quite the woman.

"But back to how I get involved. I was working in a factory and I met a union organizer. From her I learned what it was like to have a sense of control over my life. She had helped us organize ourselves at the factory. We began to make some changes. This was very threatening to men like my husband, but also to men at the union. Women were beginning to speak up and demand to be heard. I thought, if we can make changes here at the factory then we also can make changes in how we live.

"The ANC was banned, but that didn't keep us from carrying on the work. I had a neighbor who would wear something with green, yellow, and black in it when I would see her leave home two or three evenings a week. I thought she must be in ANC. I asked her one evening as she left if I might escort[9] her part of the way. As we talked, she asked if I would like to join her at her friends for a social gathering. I did. We would meet in different people's homes. We would have some beer setting around and tea, so if anyone from the neighborhood stopped by they would think we were just having a social gathering. We had to be careful because there were informers in every neighborhood.

"It was at these meetings that we learned about how to organize ourselves and to work in small groups within our neighborhood. Most people think that all ANC did was violent guerrilla-type warfare. Most of our work was very low key and within neighborhoods. The media would blow up the violent part, but that is not what the government was so worried about. They knew we had strong solid bases in the townships and that the people were being organized. Because ANC was banned, we never used its name, but the people knew who was helping them. Like back in 1978 when the women at Crossroads a squatters town in the area of Cape Town protested the demolishing of their homes—that came about because women were learning how to take the lead."

The Crossroads incident was carried on African television: "The women of Crossroads called a meeting, and in this way committees were formed. With this delegation we went to speak to the authorities. 'Why are you so hard on us?' we asked. 'We are doing no harm.' The police commissioner who heard us, didn't even bother to reply. He only showed us the paper that says Crossroads must go."[10]

Zellda continued, "Women were able to also work against the pass laws—laws requiring passes for blacks—in that they would come in from the 'homelands' to be with their husbands who worked in the cities and mines. The government did not consider our families to be families. We were just so much cheap labor. The women in the neighborhood who did not have passes would find work within the community—like child minders or beer makers or some other needed service. The other women in the community would do whatever needed to be done out of the area so the women would not have to take transport away from the relatively safe area.

"The most difficult group of women to organize were the domestics. They were very separated from their families and from each other. That was part of my job, to try to meet with the women on the days they had off and help them to find ways to get better pay and shorter hours. It was very hard because I had to win their trust and then assure them that other women were concerned about how to make some changes. We also had to be careful that the people they worked for didn't suspect that we were trying to organize them. We found a church where the women could go on their afternoons off. We had a woman there who could talk with them. This was one of our best arrangements, because it was a colored church and it looked like we were going there for Bible study. In a way we were studying the Bible, because we took to heart that Jesus did come to set the oppressed free. We were finding ways to set ourselves free.

"I want to add here that most of the women I worked with were very devout Christian women. I am sure that it is our faith that has kept most of us going. Our faith and our solidarity with each other is what has enabled us to be the women we are," Zellda assured me.

A Wise Woman Once Said

There is another woman that I have met in the literature about women in South Africa whose metaphor to describe how women must come together is a beautiful African story. Her name is Tshepo Khumbane. She is from Northern Transvaal in South Africa.

"I want to speak about how we can solve our problems so that life can be worth living," she began.

"We must build a car or wagon to transport the community to progress and development. The car or vehicle is built by you through organization. We must build this vehicle by bringing different parts together neatly and correctly fitted so that its duty may be fulfilled."

Khumbane then reminds the women that the vehicle must be safe to drive in the community. The car cannot have parts in the wrong place or a faulty engine. If it does it will never move right.

She likens the car to the community. "No, this car will never move. This car which represents your organization is dismantled by the difficulties you have just raised. 'Dikwaikwai'—pride—like the middle-class ladies in high heels. Pride in the chairlady or in the committee, who will not let other members in the club raise their views. She would say, 'Who is she? Someone like me will not talk such rubbish.' This type of woman is here with you in the group, but her attitude hinders the group's progress. She is like a bent bolt that stops the car from moving."

Khumbane compares the car and a gossipy-biting tongue. The car—community— has to be strong to overcome the weakness of the biting tongue. She questions if the women of the community can be strong.

She also suggests a direction for the women. "Don't you think it is time that we seek for our own God to show us direction? We have been praying for decades but with no solution. Is it not better we look forward for another direction to reach God? We have prayed long enough to an extent of having our knees bruised. We should ask him where our home is and to whom we belong."

Khumbane reminds the women that their children are critical of their gossipy-selfish behavior. She points out it is the biting tongue of the "me first" woman that keeps the car—community—from working together. "It is important to discuss together to plan and share, but if some are on high heels, others on three-quarters and others barefooted, we will never be able to walk together."[11]

9

Women Crossing the Line for Peace: Stories from Asia

Women do not carry the "dove" high because of some genetic make-up. Our ability to identify with marginalized people who suffer is due in part to the imperialistic maneuvering of men. We have been the "other," the marginalized—politically, economically, socially, and culturally—for generations. Men have played the role of the protector and women the protected. But today wars are not fought out on a battlefield but in villages, towns, and cities. More women and children die in wars than men. More women and children are left homeless, either within their own country or as refugees. War is no longer a game played by men, it is a killing of women and children—if not by bullets and bombs than by hunger and disease.

The Gulf War of 1990–1991 had many ramifications on the women in the region. There are many different theories as to why Iraq invaded Kuwait and why the United States was able to seduce the support of the UN and allied nations into the war. But to understand war, one needs to look not just at a particular war but at the ideology of war.

HOW THE ENEMY IS CREATED

In his book *Faces of the Enemy*, Sam Keen discusses the theology of war. "In war each nation worships itself."[1] Keen cites the connection that has been made in the "god" that serves as "the secretary of defense" and justification for war. A divine calling can come from "god," be it in the United States and our "manifest destiny," or Japan and the Great East Asia Co-Prosperity Sphere, or Hitler and the return of the Third Reich, or Mussolini and the return of the Roman Empire. "This war 'god' is a vampire who thrives on blood, is the agent of disharmony between nations."[2] Sometimes this "god" is seen in one person leading a nation, like Hitler, and other times it is a nation such as the United States that claims their national security preempts the rights of other peoples and nations. Keen suggests that the issue of war and peace is a theological issue and until this "god," which has been made by man, is killed and buried there will be no alternative to war.

To play the game of war, an enemy has to be developed. "It seems unlikely that we will have any considerable success in controlling warfare unless we come to understand the logic of political paranoia, and the process of creating propaganda that justifies our hostility," Keen says.[3] The propaganda begins with brainwashing our children. As Rodgers and Hammerstein wrote in 1949, "You've Got To Be Carefully Taught."[4] This kind of propaganda was seen soon after the war began in the Gulf. Video war games such as the *Arabian Nightmare* and *Gulf Strike* were in the stores for children. The face of the enemy was being drawn in cartoons. Hate crimes in the United States against Arab Americans increased more than 300 percent in the first half of 1991 over the last half of 1990. It is the mothers who nurture their children who must help them to learn how to counteract the myths of the media, the violence of the video, and the hate that dehumanizes the "enemy."

It is not just the horror of the death of war that women suffer, they also serve as the spoils of the conquering army. Rape and sexual abuse seem to be *"a just"* part of what men expect in war. The raping of young girls and the cutting open of pregnant women's bellies are not just tales for soldiers to brag about, but realities that women have to endure.

Women of the Middle East can tell us about how war has affected their lives and how they are working together to bring peace. Not just a political peace, of ceasefires, but peace, *shalom*, of living together in harmony and understanding.

POLITICS DIVIDE—FAITH UNITES: PALESTINE

The morning fog was still hanging along the California coast. Sunshine came late in the morning to the Monterey Bay. I pulled my jacket closer as Jean[5] and I found a quiet place under the pines. The morning ocean breeze was like an astringent to my sleepy eyes. The busy schedule of the mission conference[6] had kept both of us hopping. We had both come to the conference to be facilitators in the dialogue on the role of women and how they learn to empower themselves; she as a Palestinian woman, and I as one who had listened to women's stories from around the globe.

My knowledge and understanding of the Middle East was very limited. It wasn't until I met Ben and Carol Weir, after Ben had been released by the Shiite Muslims,[7] and came back to the United States, that I began to learn more about the Middle East. Now I am learning even more.

Jean's warm smile put me at ease as we began to talk. I was wondering how people in the Middle East related to her as a female Palestinian Christian, since most of the people there are Muslims. She told me most Americans are very ignorant about her part of the world. I wondered if she had seen through me. As we talked about her role as a female Palestinian Christian within the community and with

Palestinian women she shared some of the limitations.

She found that restrictions came more from the political aspects of life there than from either the fact that she was a woman or a Christian. Because of the oppression that the Palestinians have to suffer, she was limited in what she could do. But these limits could be overcome and they were. The women of the Middle East have worked together for peace since the Palestinians were put in camps in 1948. Though often the tensions have been high, there have also been women in small groups in the villages and communities who use their talents of negotiation and diplomacy to ease the conflict in their daily lives. The tensions have a history that includes both the Ottoman rule of 900 years since the 7th century and more recently the Balfour Declaration of 1917 and the British-French promises to the Arab nations during World War I. The litany of territorial aggression and border disputes is often forgotten: 1967, Israeli occupation of the West Bank, Golan Heights, and Gaza Strip; 1974, Turkish occupation of Northern Cyprus; 1982, Israeli invasion of southern Lebanon, and Syria's crossing the Lebanon border on the east.

As we talked about the political tensions and conflicts in the daily lives of the women in her community, Jean explained how the differences in culture and religion had helped in addressing these tensions. There is a misconception about the Arab world, that they are all Muslims. She stressed there are Christian Arabs and there are Jewish Arabs. In the Israel-Palestinian conflict, one will find women from all three faiths talking, understanding, and working together. Wars may be fought because of manmade gods, but they are not fought because of religions. Working for peace, *shalom*, in the Middle East has brought together different cultural and religious backgrounds. If one were to ask women why there are conflicts within their countries, differences in religion and culture would not be given as the reasons. The wars in the Middle East are over land and resources and national security, not over Christian, Jewish, or Muslim beliefs. Muslims, Jews, and Christians all look to the same God as their creator, thus they have a basis from which to build. She also stressed the common need to provide a home for their children. Community and social welfare are things they are all interested in. The women look for ways to meet the daily needs of their families. They talk and work as individual women yet together. The women understand that they all have feelings, needs, joys, and sorrows. They see the commonalities, not the differences. They look for understanding, not animosity. They know that some have to suffer more, but those who suffer less are still able to understand the others' pain and be in solidarity with them.

It has been the women's popular committees that have been the backbone of the Palestinian community. Because of the detention of hundreds of men, women are left to be the providers of the family. Usually there is no income and often times not a home or even shelter. The women have organized themselves to meet the daily needs of education for the children, income, child care, and food. They are not formally organized; they just work together to meet their needs.

As we talked about the Gulf War, Jean helped me to understand even more what solidarity among women can really mean. I learned that the Gulf War did not stop the Israeli women's (Women in Black) support of the Palestinian women's efforts. This is not to say that there was not greater stress and tension, but they did continue. The "Women in Black" continued their weekly silent vigils protesting Israel's occupation of Palestinian territories. They suffered harassment, physical abuse. The police no longer protected them once the Gulf War began.

The women realize that it is time for dialogue and working together cooperatively to heal the open wounds that have been there for decades, wounds that come when one nation dominates another, wounds that are hard to heal. Jean implied it will be women who will lead the way in this healing process. Like any wound, for it to heal properly it has to heal from the inside out, and that is the way women work. Women work with the people, the women and children, and some men. When communities are healed, then countries can be healed.

Our ruptured world will find this kind of healing when people have faces and when communication allows for cooperation, compassion, consensus, and community.

WOMEN TAKE THE LEAD: PHILIPPINES

The women of the Philippines are well organized. It was their strong leadership that made it possible for Corazon Aquino to be elected president and Ferdinand Marcos to be ousted. How did the women develop that much power?

Beth and I crossed paths often between 1985 and 1987. We would see each other at the library at the Graduate Theology Union (GTU) in Berkeley, California, where we both were studying for our Masters of Divinity, or on the campus of the Pacific School of Religion (PSR). When I became involved in the Church Network on the Philippines (CNOP) we became friends. Often Beth and I discussed what was happening in the Philippines. I soon realized that Beth was teaching me about the women in her country as we chatted on the benches in front of the library, over a meal at a CNOP meeting, or in the PACTS (Pacific Asian Center for Theology and Strategies) office on the PSR campus. I often attended meetings where she would be speaking about the changes that were coming in her country.

One day I had asked Beth about the herstory of women in the Philippines. She told me, "There is a long herstory of women empowering themselves. Being under colonial rule, first Spain then the United States set the tone for women to be subservient and docile. Yet in the 1700s a woman general, Josefa Gabriela Silang, was not willing to be either of these things and became a model and standard bearer for the women of the Philippines.

"It is this spirit that we saw in Lorena Barros in the 1970s. Her friends called her Laurie. As a student at the University of the Philippines, Laurie became involved with student teach-ins. Her vitality and leadership made it possible for her to organize MAKIBAKA (Free Movement of New Women) in 1970. This was a unique group of women. They were the first to include the liberation of women, from the male and class oppression, with the liberation of the nation. Barros spoke out on this issue. I will give you a book that will help you to learn more about our struggle."

Beth gave me the *Sourcebook on Philippine Women in Struggle*. One of Barros's quotes in the book illustrates what Beth was talking about. "The oppression of women in the Philippine society cannot be isolated from the oppressive character of society as a whole. Since the Filipino women are fundamental to the Filipino condition, their oppression reflects a fundamentally oppressive system of social relationships."[8]

Beth continued, "The short life of MAKIBAKA—it was declared illegal in 1972 when Marcos established martial law—didn't diminish the work that it started. They had protested the national beauty contest in 1970. Their attack on the commercialization of sex brought them national recognition. They carried their campaign to the factories, barrios, and working communities. Barros was a scholar and she equipped the women with an understanding of how historically women became oppressed. MAKIBAKA used education as a means to enlighten women about their rights and helped them to empower themselves both in the home and in the work place. By the time MAKIBAKA was made illegal, they had reached women in the rural mountains, the city slums, the work place, and the homes of the middle class. She was twenty-eight years old when she was wounded and later died from gunshots from a military ambush on March 24, 1976. She was the light that lit the torch that has been passed on through the years."

We picked up this conversation at another time. "Can you tell me the herstory of GABRIELA and its goals or objective? From what I have read it sounds like they were well organized."

"GABRIELA really stands for two things. It is the name of a woman general who fought along side of her husband in the 1790's against the Spaniards. When he was killed she carried on. She has been a symbol for the women of the Philippines every since. But it also stands for General Assembly Binding Women for Reform, Integrity, Equality, Leadership, and Action. This coalition brought women from many different sectors together in 1984. It was the first step towards the engathering of over fifty women's groups from social, political, religious, ethnic, regional, and economic background. With the first assembly held in March of 1984 the resurgence of the women's movement in the Philippines was began. After Marcos's marshall law began in 1972 small groups of women in their region or work area met and strategized ways to assert their rights through boycotts, stage-ins, strikes, and rallies.

"GABRIELA set forth four basic principles: (1) to restore democracy, (2) to allow women to be equal partners with men in decision making, (3) to enhance the development of women, and (4) to eliminate all forms of oppression of women.

"It is these basic principles that give the focus to the women's movement. Democracy for our country had to come before we would have our freedom, but we were not going to lose sight of the oppressive nature of society that restricted women. This was the foundation, the strong and powerful leadership, women's power, the linchpin of the liberation movement. On March 8th, 1985, at the

International Women's Day Rally we proclaimed 'A Nation Can Never Be Free Unless Its Own Women Are Free.' We had our 'woman.' Cory became our president. She had come from a wealthy family, but she had suffered with the poor under the harsh rule of Marcos."

The last time I talked with Beth she was gravely concerned about the direction her country was taking. Cory had not been the champion of the poor and the women that she said she would be. "I am not sure it is so much Cory or the fact that the military is still very powerful and she does not control them. Also the U.S. government cannot keep its finger out of the pie. It wants to keep their bases there and the people want them out. I am not sure just what is going to happen."

They had their woman, but she turned out to be repressive. The human rights abuses began to climb. One of the targets was the church workers, as they worked among the poor both in the rural areas and in the urban slums. The former U.S. Attorney General and international human rights lawyer, Ramsey Clark, along with five others—a twenty-five-year veteran of the CIA, a catholic Sister, a lawyer, a writer, and a history professor—led a fact-finding mission to the Philippines in May 1987. In their report they documented violations of human rights: how the military backed death squads and how right-wing, anticommunist vigilante groups roamed the countryside terrorizing villages; how these groups were covertly supported by the government; and how the U.S. CIA was engaged in low intensity conflict (LIC) similar to that in Central America.

My involvement in the Filipino community in the San Francisco Bay area helped me to keep up on the struggles of the people in the Philippines. Knowing part of the struggle in the Philippines and other developing countries with the debt crisis, I went to Washington, DC, to take part in an education-lobbying meeting on the debt crisis. We were there to discuss the debt crisis, then lobby both the IMF and the World Bank at their annual meeting.

I had seen Professor Leonor Briones when she was introduced to the conference, but sharing an evening meal with her allowed me to get to know her as a person. A small woman with the energy of ten, she founded the Freedom from Debt Coalition in the Philippines. Her slightly graying hair could be a reflection the stress of her dedication to her mission of telling people of the unjust and immoral debts that burden the Philippines and other developing countries.

As we waited for the Metro to take us back to our lodgings, Leonor shared some of her thoughts with me about the burden of the debt. She explained that women are the hardest hit. They are the first not to have work and to see the effects of no health care. There was both a sadness and anger on her face as she told about how girls have to leave school because of the lack of space, books, and teachers. But her usual light shone in her eyes as she spoke of how women are very innovative, finding ways to work together, pooling their talents and their time and supporting each other in their suffering. She explained how it was easier to get women to protest and to make their concerns known.

She told about gatherings and rallies: they march with banners; they have groups to go to local government officials and sometimes send people to the capital. She also explained that it is not as easy to travel there as it is in the United States and sometimes it is very dangerous to protest. The anger returned to her face as she pointed out that more money went to the World Bank and IMF and the United States than they received in aid. I knew that was why it was time for the women to speak out.

Leonor and I have corresponded over the years and things have not changed that much. The poor and especially the women are still carrying the burden of the country and the natural disasters of typhoons, earthquakes, and volcanos have added to their problems. The government is not able or is unwilling to address the needs of the poor.

The women of the Philippines still carry on the movement. They are educating women about their rights and fighting the influence of the TNC's in the free-trade zones, sex tourism, and debt payment. All of these are exploiting women, and the struggle continues against both the economic and cultural oppression. There is still work to be done on the last three of the GABRIELA principles. Until women are empowered and have equality in decision making, the women's movement will not lack for work.

10

Women and Revolution: Stories from Latin America and the Caribbean

SEEING PEACE THROUGH THE EYES OF WOMEN: CUBA

In the spring of 1987, I attended the Third Continental Congress and General Assembly of the Christian Peace Conference of Latin America and the Caribbean (CPCLAC) in Havana. I went as an observer delegate and part of the press corps for the *Sequoia* newspaper of the Northern California Ecumenical Council. This latter role afforded me the opportunity to interview delegates and come to know the Cuban media. Separation of church and state in Cuba has not been a totally repressive arrangement, but has allowed the church to stand outside the state and give constructive criticism. The church is listened to there and thus has a kind of influence that we lack in the United States. An example of the Cuban openness to listening was presented when I was interviewed on Cuban TV about my faith. The complete interview with no cuts, voiceovers, or censoring was run on the evening news. Which nationwide network in the United States would even bother to interview a seminary student from Cuba, let alone carry the full unedited interview?

While in Cuba, I was able to visit schools, hospitals, prisons, and cultural events. There were papers presented by women and discussion groups on women's issues related to peace. I want to share some stories I heard and impressions I had of these women, not just from Cuba but throughout Latin America and the Caribbean.

One of the first woman I met was Sophia. She was a member of the Reformed Presbyterian Church of Cuba and worked with women who were battered in their homes. She and I had agreed to meet on the second evening of the conference. I was sitting on a bench looking out at the sea when she came up the path that ran along the sea wall. The evening light turned her white hair even more silvery.

Her pace had slowed and there was a grace to her walk. With her head tilted to balance the smile on her face she greeted me with a hug as I rose from the bench.

"I wanted to talk with you about the role of women here in Cuba," I said, "not just in the church, but in the country and in the revolution."

"Women were involved in the struggle and fighting before independence on January 1, 1959," Sophia explained. "They have been even more involved in the restructuring of the country. Our women were illiterate and we began a literacy campaign to teach not just the women but the men also to read and write."

"That sounds like the campaign I learned about in Nicaragua last summer," I interjected.

"Yes, they knew ours was wonderfully successful and they copied our program. We were able to increase the literacy rate over fifty percent in just six months. Young girls and boys from the city went into the rural areas and mountains and lived with the families in villages and worked with them and taught them. We soon realized that women needed more than just to be able to read and write, so schools were started for them. Most of these women were mothers and they were concerned about health needs."

"How did the women address those needs?" I asked. "In Zambia, hospitals that had been for whites only were made available for the Africans. Are the hospitals that were just for the wealthy before independence now open for all the people?"

"Yes, but they are in the cities. Our greatest need was for rural health care. Again it was women who responded to this need. They organized themselves and came into Havana and were given the initial training in basic public health and first aid. Each month they are given additional training as midwives, in nutrition, child illnesses, and pre- and postnatal care. At the same time the university is training more doctors, both women and men," Sophia explained with pride. She herself is a professional women, an educator, and a 1960 graduate of the University of Santa Clara.

"Is there a feminist movement or women's movement in Cuba?" I asked.

"No, not like you have in the United States. A year and half after Independence, on August 23, 1960, the Federation of Cuban Women (FCW) was formed. It was important for us to organize. As often happens, the women fight and struggle side-by-side with the men in the revolution, then when victory comes we get sent back to the home." Sophia's eyes were now glowing with excitement. She had said before that since she became professor of sociology at the University of Santa Clara in 1961 she would not want to be without her work.

"What are some professions that women are in now that they were not in before the revolution?"

"A few of the wealthy women went to college or, as in my case, got some financial help, but most women did not even finish primary school—if they went to school at all. Now women are free and are encouraged to study whatever they want. We need all the well-trained persons we can get. Women are not discriminated against when it comes to schooling. Some people wonder if Christians are able to attend institutions of higher education or if students have to be members of the Communist Party. We can and we do not. I will say that sometimes it is harder to get into more popular courses but there are Christian women and men in higher education." (The following Sunday at church I met a young woman who was studying to pass her bar exam and a young man who was studying medicine.)

I was interested in knowing how Sophia saw the women of Cuba involved in the peace movement. "We are here to discuss the issues of peace in this part of the world. What role have the women of Cuba played since January 1959 in peace in the world?"

"I am sure you will agree with me that peace is not just the absence of war or overt conflict. For there to be true peace, *shalom*, everyone's basic needs must be met—work, food, shelter, clothing, education, health, recreation, and participation in decision making. We take this kind of peace very seriously here. That is what we fought for and that is what we are working for. We support all peoples in having these basic needs met. I think women are more sensitive to these needs because they have to deal with them every day. We have had women go to other countries and help with literacy campaigns. We have sent women doctors, teachers, and engineers to train other women and men. Most of all, we have been the leaders in training our own children and each other in understanding the importance of respect and love and working together to build community. The women of Cuba have been the leaders in our country in peace—building in the family, community, and even in our nation."[1]

As we got up to return to the evening festivities, I thought about what Sophia had said and wondered how the propaganda in my country about Cuba could be checked.

LIBERATION AND PEACE GO HAND IN HAND: BRAZIL

We had all had a very long day, with hours of sitting. Marie and I were ready for a little walk to stretch our legs. We had listened to a talk that morning on "Liberation and Peace from Women's Perspective" at the CPCLAC. As we stepped outside of the convention center, we were able to feel the breeze from the sea. Havana is a beautiful city.

Marie is from Brazil. Her black hair frames her face, which is dominated by sparkling black eyes. They are intense, warm—the kind of warmth that I find so often in women who have an inner strength. It is a strength that carries them through their struggles and suffering.

"We heard this morning about the way history is written and that herstory is not part of what we read," I began. "I was wondering about how the women in your country are writing herstory today."

"Our government has moved from the colonialism of Portugal to the new colonialism of the United States. We have moved from feudalism to capitalism. The government seems to think that just because capitalism worked for you in the United States it will work for us. (I am not sure it works all that well for you but we will not get into that at this point.) Making money and paying off the debt is more important than caring for and providing for the people, the poor—the majority being women and children. We have had to do without health care, jobs and job training, schooling, food, shelter, the basic necessities for life. Women realize that they cannot count on the menfolk of the families to provide for them, so they have organized themselves to get the government to provide services such as water, sewage, market areas, schools, and clinics."

"If the government has not provided them in the past why are they doing it now?" I asked.

"Before, the men in the local government thought women would just accept what they said, and therefore the local officials pocketed the money that was to be spent on these things. The women in a barrio of Sao Paulo found out what was happening and they organized a rally, inviting the local officials. When the officials got there, the women of the community confronted them with the facts they had gotten from higher offices in the government. They also presented the officials with a priority list and a time schedule of when to have each project done. They offered to provide some of the labor to complete the projects."

"What were the projects listed?"

"The top one was piped-in water. The women had a grid for where the standpipes were to go. They offered to dig the trenches and to lay the pipe, but the government had to provide the materials and connect it with the main water line. The second item was a building that could be used for a clinic, school, church, and recreation. The women had drawn up plans and again were willing to provide some of the labor. The government would equip the rooms for the clinic, school, and recreation, and the women would provide the staff. They had already found a nurse who was willing to come three days a week from a church hospital and one of the Sisters from the convent was willing to teach the children with the help of some of the high-school students from their school."

"It sounds like the women were very well organized," I commented.

"They were, and the men were so surprised that they had trouble at first realizing what was happening. A woman named Carla, who was a very forceful person, pressed them until they agreed there in front of about 500 women that they would use the money for these things. See, we had already gotten the assurance of the money from a higher level."

"What is happening today? Do they have their standpipes and their building?" I inquired.

"Yes, and even better, Carla ran for the local office and won. Women had done such a great job of getting the improvements and showing how the local officials were corrupt that even the men voted for her."

The sun was getting low in the sky as we walked back to the convention center to board the van back to the hotel. I felt Marie, with her slender grace and strong presence, was also a force to be reckoned with when it came to women finding their own liberation leading to a new peace and dignity that has not been theirs in the past.

WE WILL FIND OUR SONS: CENTRAL AMERICA

In 1986 it was no longer low intensity conflict (LIC) in Central America, There were killings, torturings, bombings, and disappearances. My roommate, Betty, woke me in the night in Jinotega, Nicaragua, and asked if those were gun shots she was hearing. We decided they were, but they were not getting closer. We had already had our suitcases searched in San Salvador, while we were out of our hotel room. When the fact-finding study group we were with went to the offices of the *Co-Madres* (Committees of Mothers of the Disappeared) in San Salvador, El Salvador, we found that it had been partially destroyed by a bomb a few days before. We were experiencing some of the ramifications of LIC.

While at the *Co-Madres* we talked with Andrea, a mother of two girls, who were playing at her feet, and a son, twelve years old, who had disappeared from their field in the eastern part of the country.

"How do you know he was taken?" our translator asked.

"We found one of his sandals and drops of blood at the end of the row of corn he had been hoeing. My husband disappeared three weeks before my son," she told us.

"Why are you here in San Salvador? It is a long way from your home in the mountains above San Miguel?" my roommate Betty asked.

"I came here because I had heard that they could help me find my husband and son. I was afraid to stay there," she said. Her eyes seemed to have cried all the tears she had, but a sorrow that only a loss like hers could bring remained on her face.

"What are you afraid of?" asked Lew, one of the men with us.

"The army thinks we are part of the FMLN[2] and have even taken women and children when they are not able to get the information they want from the men and the boys."

"How have the *Co-Madres* helped you since you came to San Salvador?" I asked.

"They sent people to the army, police, treasury police, and have had their people in San Miguel looking also. They helped me to find work and provided child care when I am able to work," Andrea said. There was a faint smile on her face when she talked about her work.

"What kind of work do you do?" Betty asked.

"I make things to sell like this," she said as she held up a beautiful cloth that would serve as a communion cloth in a church. "I also make clothes for children and shirts for men. We have a cooperative here that does this kind of work."

We learned that the women have been able to find some of the disappeared in jails, but more often than not they find them in shallow graves along the side of the road, or on a garbage heap. The work of the *Co-Madres* is something I am not sure I could do. They hope that even in cases where blood was found at the site of the disappearance, they will find those who have been kidnapped alive.

We found similar stories repeated in Guatemala and Nicaragua. Women are not allowing the government to totally control their lives by taking their sons, brothers, and husbands. They are fighting back. The oppression of the poor by the powerful wealthy has taken on a political element when the oppression is expressed in deaths, disappearances, and intimidation.

CONCLUSION

The women of Latin America have had to struggle against the colonialism of Spain and Portugal, and now they struggle against the ideology of capitalism backed by the United States and enforced by U.S.-supported terrorism. When any ideology does not provide for mutual growth and shared decision making but instead dominates; when an ideology does not allow for the basic necessities of life but instead exploits the people; when an ideology does not allow for the dignity of persons but instead oppresses them; then that ideology is destructive. The women of Latin America are working from a positive ideology, that all people have basic rights and those rights are shared in family and community, in nation and worldwide. They are determined to become part of the policy formation in various levels of their government.

11

Working for Peace in Many Ways:
Stories from the United States

PIECES TO PEACE

It was a hot muggy July day that only the Midwest can produce. As I emerged from the cool terminal into the oppressive humidity of the late afternoon I saw a placard that read, "Welcome Peggy Andrews." The expectant faces of the welcoming committee turned to surprise as I walked toward them. "Are you Peggy Andrews, from Zambia," one of the women asked. I had arrived in Indianapolis to help brief the women from South Africa who had come to attend the Church Women United, 1984, Global Gathering, Ecumenical Assembly, "Come! Build a New Earth: Pieces to Peace," at Purdue University.

"Yes, I am. I returned from Zambia six weeks ago."

With still a questioning tone to her voice, Millie stated, "We thought because you were from Zambia that you would be black. That goes to show we must not make assumptions. Welcome to Indianapolis."

The next morning I met the same surprised looks when the women from South Africa were introduced to me. They also thought I would be black. Ethel, the head of the South African delegation, told me she wondered why a delegate from Zambia was going to be the hostess on the trip up to Purdue. After a briefing at a church we boarded a bus and set off for a wonderful five days of talking and acting for peace.

As we rode through the lush green cornfields of Indiana, the South African women told me they could not believe that the corn would be fed to cattle, hogs, and chickens. "We have children starving because we cannot get corn to feed them and you waste this on pigs!" declared Ethel.

I knew her frustration. I had seen starvation in Zambia and East Africa, also in India and other parts of Asia. We would soon hear even more about how hunger can take away peace in a family and nation.

The power of the women gathering at Purdue was a fitting cap to my travels of the last three years. I had listened to women tell their stories as we sat under mango trees in Zambia and mended their fishing baskets; under ceiba trees in Thailand and stripped kapok from the trees pods; in a bamboo grove in Taiwan and watched them weave. The voices all coming together provided a spirit, compelling and liberating.

One of the greatest celebrations of women working for peace came Friday evening during the worship service. This service focused on our commitment to World Day of Prayer and the Fellowship of the Least Coin. It ended with the Ribbon of Peace. Each of these rituals have a humbleness about them that brings forth the power of women.

WORLD DAY OF PRAYER

In 1887 the women in the Presbyterian Church in the United States sent out a call for a day of prayer for missions. Thus the seed was planted that grew into the World Day of Prayer. Now on the first Friday of March each year women around the globe gather in small villages, dorm rooms, great cathedrals, and ordinary churches to pray for peace and reconciliation. For most Christian women, this is a time when they know that they will be touching hearts with sisters around the world.

It is not just Christian women who join in. While I was in Thailand (1984), a woman in a village out of Chiang Mai told me about a Buddhist friend who joined her and some of her Christian sisters in her home for World Day of Prayer that year. "My friend wants peace also. She asked if she could come and pray with us for peace. How could I tell her no? Jesus welcomed everyone; so must we."

The Friday evening worship service at the CWU Gathering helped us to gain a sense of sisterhood, as the international delegates gathered on the stage. Each of us was dressed in the traditional dress of our country. As my friend Joyce Tembo from Zambia told her story, I hoped the lights did not reflect off the tears that were marking my face. She told of the girls who had not been able to attend school and how the women in the communities were working to provide literacy classes for the girls and themselves.

A woman from Korea helped us to see the suffering of families that were split because of the division in her country. Women of Trinidad and Brazil told of the pain that women suffer in their regions due to capitalism's lack of concern for the needs of the poor. We heard of the tension in the Middle East. A mother of the Pacific Islands pleaded for a stop to the nuclear testing that was producing "jelly babies." Our hearts and spirits were touched as each story and prayer bonded our sisterhood.

The World Day of Prayer is held in 170 countries and regions. This movement brings together women of various races, cultures, and traditions in close fellowship, understanding, and action throughout the year.

THE FELLOWSHIP OF THE LEAST COIN

In her deep red silk dress of traditional Thai styling, Boonmee Julkiree, who had been my hostess while I was in Bangkok, Thailand, approached the microphone. As she stepped up on the riser, her petite size did not keep the women from seeing the commitment in her face. Her gentle voice helped to soothe the tears that had come from hearing the stories just told. Boonmee inspired us to appreciate the simpleness and yet the power of women collectively pursuing peace through prayer, as she interpreted the logo for the Fellowship of the Least Coin: The lotus flower made by praying hands. The 2,300 women in attendance listened and remembered the power they had felt when they participated in this fellowship in their own communities.[1]

In 1956, a group of Christian women in the United States had been concerned because of the bitterness that still existed between the nations involved in World War II. An international fellowship team of reconciliation was formed to travel to Japan, Korea, Hong Kong, and the Philippines. When it came time for them to get visas for Korea, Shanti Solomon from India was denied one, along with the woman from Japan. There was much discussion about whether the tour should continue without them. "No! go along," Shanti urged. "I want to ponder this matter in my heart. I shall wait for you in Manila with our Christian friends there, studying to see if perhaps I myself have wrong thoughts." The tour did continue, and Shanti went to the Philippines to wait for the other women. While there a beautiful lotus flower opened for her.

My friend Shirin Samuel, the executive secretary of the Fellowship of the Least Coin, shared with me the story of this lotus flower in a small booklet she wrote.

> As Shanti searched for her answer, she was reading the story of the good Samaritan (in the Bible), who succored the man who fell among thieves. She saw, "We village women in India have drawn away our skirts from the terrible suffering of war-torn mothers and children, everywhere. We have been like the priest who passed by on the other side, saying smugly, 'This is not our business.' What can I do now to bring together all those women who have been so badly hurt?"
>
> She was still pondering while she and the group of women in the Manila church read together the gospel of Mark.
>
> The widow's mite,[2] that's the answer, you have to give yourself along with your Least Coin. Real giving is a throwing off our pride. Only when our hearts are empty of self can God fill them with love and forgiveness. Why could we not start a fellowship where all women, any woman, shall pray for one another in a different land? There must be some concrete symbol of her concern, possibly the smallest coin of her country? Like the widow's mite, to help people who are sick or in trouble.
>
> How humiliating it is to always be on the receiving end as we are in Asia. It is important that rich and poor, educated and illiterate, can give on the same level, Shanti explained to the tour women when they

arrived in Manila.

When the invitation was later extended to other Christian women in North and South America, Australia, Europe, and Africa, they gladly joined the Fellowship of the Least Coin.[3]

Now again in a global meeting women were praying for peace, justice, and reconciliation. As the international delegation passed out small medallions with the lotus flower on one side and the praying circle (the logo for the World Day of Prayer) on the other, there was a spirit-filled hush in the Music Hall at Purdue. This spirit led us in the Peace Ribbon procession.

THE RIBBON OF PEACE

In March of 1982 Justine Merritt, a peace-loving mother in Denver, Colorado, had what she thought was a "foolish" notion to do something about the direction our country was taking toward nuclear war. She thought, "What if we create prayerfully a long, narrow length of fabric with illustrations of what people could not bear to lose through nuclear war?" Her "foolish" idea caught on, and not just the one mile that she first envisioned but miles of ribbon were sewn. As the idea spread so did the ribbon. Each panel of the ribbon, three feet by one-and-a-half feet, told a story of what peace meant to the person who made it. There were 20,000 panels, done by children at summer programs and church schools, by women and men in senior centers, that represented peace in the family, school, church, community, and peace in one's own life. For instance, in Tucson, Arizona, a miniature Pentagon was placed in the plaza of the federal building with peace marchers encircling it with their part of the ribbon. On August 6, 1985, women and men, children and youth, over 100,000 strong, gathered in Washington, DC, to demonstrate their desire for peace in memory of the bombing of Japan. The ribbon encircled the Pentagon and extended beyond.

And now the women at the conference were streaming out of the Music Hall and down the streets of the campus singing, carrying candles and their portion of the ribbon.

This was a night of sisterhood, of global sisterhood for peace, justice, and reconciliation. Women calling for prayer, an Indian woman realizing that all women can be together and share the least, and a mother wanting a life full of peace, *shalom,* for her children have made a difference in this world.

THE JAPANESE PEACE CRANE IN JAIL

The sun was not up yet as we got out of the cars. A group of us from my home church in Berkeley, California, was going to the sunrise worship service on Good Friday. I had come the two Easters I had been in the Bay Area, but this time was different. I was going to do moral obedience.[4] As we crossed the road and gathered at the edge of a field we could hear the soft singing and guitar music in the background. As each person spoke or led us in prayer we were aware that down the road a half-mile at Lawrence Livermore Labs, nuclear weapons were being designed. Was there to be no end to the militarism of the United States? We had enough bombs to blow up the earth forty times or more. When was enough, enough?

After prayers and songs, scriptures and meditations—some by Christians, some by Jews, some by Buddhists—those of us who were going to do moral obedience began to block the intersection. I was afraid. I had visited the state prison at San Quentin and a federal prison in Richmond, Virginia, but I had never been to jail. I found a place between two women I knew, each of whom had been arrested before. As we knelt, prayed, and held hands, I knew what I was doing was right. As each person was arrested for blocking the street and led to the waiting buses, our names were called out and cheers of support came forth. After a long wait and ride, we arrived at the county jail. There we were given brown-bag lunches as we were stripped of all our personal effects, even wedding rings.

The women were in one holding cell and the men in the one next to it. Almost immediately Joyce, one of the protestors, asked for a pail of water and a scrub brush. She told the guard she would gladly scrub the toilets for them. Soon we had clean toilets. When the toilet paper ran out, Bernice produced a large supply from her ample bosoms. Jan and Mary took off the cloth wraps that had been worn as skirts over their shorts and made curtains, so we could have privacy. With our personal needs met, we began conversing, giving back rubs, and singing.

I had found a place on a bench against the wall where I could watch and listen to the others. After we had eaten our lunches, Marilyn tore a square piece of paper and started to fold it into a crane. I knew what she was doing, as did the others. Soon all of us were making cranes. By this time I had chatted with one of the male guards. I walked over to the bars that separated the holding cell from the corridor and called to Tom. He came over.

"I would like to give you this peace crane," I said as I handed him the small crane through the bars. I had made mine small, because I had found a pencil under the bench and had used my lunch bag to write notes of my feelings and what I was hearing.

"What is a peace crane?" Tom asked.

What a wonderful time to tell him the story! I thought. "When the atomic bombs were dropped on Japan, there was a two-year-old girl named Sadako Sasaki. Her grandmother was killed by the bomb on Hiroshima. She grew up to be a bright and energetic child. Her passion was running. She was never still. She ran to school, she ran to her friend Chizuko's home. The two girls were inseparable.

"When Sadako became ill with leukemia, 'the atomic-bomb disease;' and had to remain in the hospital, Chizuko brought Sadako a gift. 'What am I to do with a piece of gold paper and a pair of scissors?' Sadako asked.

"Chizuko smiled at her and told her the story of the Thousand Cranes. 'You take this paper and cut a square. Then you fold it and fold it until you have a crane. You remember the story about how the crane lives for a thousand years. If you fold one thousand paper cranes the gods will grant you your wish and make you well again. Here is you first crane. I have brought you more paper so you can begin now and get better soon.'

"Sadako made cranes each day and she did get better and was able to go home for awhile, but then she had to go back to the hospital. Her brother had hung all the cranes she had made from the ceiling in her room. She made six hundred forty-four before she died on October 25, 1955. Her friends and classmates folded three hundred fifty-six more cranes so that she would be buried with one thousand cranes.

"There is a monument to her and all the children who have died because of the bombs in Hiroshima Peace Park. On top of the monument is a statue of Sasako holding a golden crane. Each year on Peace Day, August 6th, children hang garlands of paper cranes on the statue. Inscribed on the monument is, 'This is our cry, this is our prayer, Peace in the world.'[5]

"So you see Tom, the peace crane is the symbol for no more atomic bombs. That is what we asked for. That is why we are here today. We want the production for annihilation stopped. We women have children and grandchildren. We want a world where they do not have to live in fear of total destruction."

With a thoughtful look in his eyes and a furrowed brow Tom responded, "I had never heard that story. When I heard that a bunch of 'peaceniks' was being brought in I was expecting a bunch of hippies. Most of you women are older than I am."

"Tom," I said, "most of us are just average citizens, working at whatever we do. If anything sets us apart it is that we feel we must do something to stop this ridiculous arms race. No one, nothing, can survive a nuclear war."

"What is your name?" Tom asked.

"Peggy, Peggy Andrews."

"Thank you Peggy, for both the crane and the story. Thank you for telling me about why you all are here. I guess if anything is worth getting arrested for, it would be to stop a nuclear war." Tom smiled as he answered his page to go to the office.

Tom walked past the cell several times that afternoon, always with a warm smile. It wasn't long until other guards came up and asked us for cranes and wanted to hear Sadako's story.

PART III

OUR BODIES ARE OUR OWN

12

Violence Against Women

The exploitation of women and their bodies has taken many different forms over the centuries and throughout different cultures. As we know, the "oldest profession" is a profession of exploitation of women—prostitution. Young girls are used in prostitution everywhere. The cruelty does not stop there. Women suffer from female genital mutilation in parts of Africa and the Middle East. In Latin American countries husbands kill their wives for honor, for machismo. In the United States a woman is raped every three minutes, and one is battered every fifteen seconds. The violence continues.

Because of the prevalence of discrimination against women and because much of that discrimination leads to violence—sexual harassment, sexual assault, rape, torture, and many different forms of domestic violence—women around the world called forth in 1979 the United Nations Convention on the Elimination of All Forms of Discrimination Against Women. This action represented the culmination of more than sixteen years of effort in which the U.S. representatives were active participants. Even though the United States signed the Convention in Copenhagen, it has not been ratified by the Senate or signed by any President since Carter.

Some have asked why should the United States sign the Convention. "By becoming a party to the Convention, a State makes an international commitment to the principle of the dignity and worth of all its citizens and to the eradication of all discrimination that precludes women from the enjoyment of their human rights and fundamental freedoms. The legal obligations under the Convention are threefold: first, the convention addresses the removal of discriminatory laws and obstacles to equality; second, it promotes equality by affirmative action; and third, it aims at eliminating attitudes, conduct, prejudices and practices that are based on the inferiority or superiority of either sex."[1] Is the United States unwilling to give the majority of their citizens these rights? We hear cries from Washington against human rights abuses in other countries and the Senate and Congress promote the respect for human rights through the Foreign Assistance Act, yet the Senate is not willing to join the one hundred and eleven plus countries in signing the Convention.

Until human rights include women's rights, the kinds of violence against women as related in the stories in the following chapters will continue. Women spoke out at the UN Conference on Human Rights in Austria in 1993 and the Fourth UN World Conference on Women in China in 1995 stating "Women's Rights are Human Rights and Human Rights are Women's Rights." We saw how women are the leaders in the nonviolent peace movements. We are now seeing them taking the leadership in speaking out for their rights and women working to eliminate violence against themselves.

These stories will be difficult to read. As I wrote them I had to stop, sometimes for days, because of the pain I felt again with my sisters. But as when I first heard the stories, I grew in strength with my sisters. Just as there is pain in giving life, so there is pain in growing in life.

CUTTING TO SAVE FOR MARRIAGE

In parts of Africa and the Middle East women are "saved" for their husbands through female genital mutilation (FGM), a common practice in twenty-eight African countries. The World Health Organization (WHO) estimates there are two million young girls each year who suffer FGM, for a total of over 100 million girls and women in the world today.[2]

Female genital mutilation ranges from circumcision, where the clitoris is removed, to total infibulation, the complete removal of all external organs and sewing the vagina closed. Religion is not a factor in this tradition. It is designed to ensure virginity at the time of marriage and to suppress the sexuality of women.

Nigeria, Ethiopia, Egypt, the Sudan, and Kenya are the countries where three-fourths of the women have experienced FGM. Eighty percent of all girls in Djibouti, Somalia, Eritrea, Ethiopia, Sierra Leone, and the Sudan are thought to have suffered FGM, some as early as at the age of two. Most girls are between eight and ten years of age when they experience FGM. This practice is coming to the United States as families immigrate from countries where it is part of their culture.

The health problems related to female genital mutilation are many and severe—hemorrhage, tetanus, sepsis, fistula, HIV/AIDS, infections of the bladder and urinary tract, difficulty in menstruation, obstructed labor during childbirth, sterilization, and even death. The emotional scars are much harder to detect. After learning more about it from the women in Kenya (see chapter 13), it became clear to me how indelible is the mark it leaves on girls and women.

Through the Inter-African Committee for the Elimination of Traditional Harmful Practices and with the help of WHO, governmental and private organizations are addressing the issue of female genital mutilation. Through education they try to persuade both women and men that the practice must be abolished. Women who have suffered from FGM are taking the lead.

CHILDREN FOR PLEASURE

Prostitution, the oldest profession in the world, has taken on a different character. While there have always been the "spoils of war" (slave prostitutes), the brothels of frontier towns, camp followers around military bases, and modern-day call girls, the women who filled these roles were usually in their late teens and early twenties. But today men do not just walk down around the corner or across the railroad tracks, or take a taxi to the redlight district, or drive to the known strips in town for streetwalkers. No! Today they get on a jet and fly to Asia or some other exotic place and take their pleasures not with young women, but with small girls.

Dame Nita Barrow, past president of World Council of Churches, from Barbados, W.I., makes the following statement regarding the changing character of prostitution: "Previous assumptions were that prostitution tourism was a phenomenon of certain parts of the world. Research and further study show that it is much more widespread than originally envisaged. In some areas it has been the exploitation of young girls and women often lured from their villages and rural homes with the promise of jobs in big cities and towns."[3]

Child prostitution is big business. Sex tourism is not officially promoted by governments, yet many an official has developed a sore neck looking the other way while having his hand warmed with dollars, deutsche marks, pounds, yen, and currency from other industrializing countries. Over one million children are involved in eight Asian countries alone, and that is not counting the children in Latin America and Africa. Young boys are part of this number, but the majority are girls, some as young as nine years old. UNICEF'S 1994 report *The Progress of Nations* lists thirty-two countries where sexual abuse of children by foreign visitors—businessmen or tourists, from inside or outside the region—has been reported.[4]

One of the most infamous places for prostitution is Olongapo City, in the Philippines. It is just outside the gates of the former U.S. Subic Bay Naval Station. The closing of the naval station and U.S. Clark Air Base has not really put a dent in the business of prostitution in the Philippines. The emphasis has merely shifted to offering sex tourism to businessmen, sending young girls to Japan to work as "waitresses," and providing mail-order brides. When I visited Thailand I did not expect to be confronted with this issue. My eyes were opened and my heart saddened as my gut became angry.

You will read of how women are working in Bangkok to end these practices and of the circumstances that lead families into selling their daughters into prostitution in chapter 14.

THE BURNING OF BEAUTY

Worldwide, the value of a wife is often counted in the amount of work she can do, the number of sons she can produce, and her ability to be a good hostess. But when her value is based on the amount of dowry—money and material things—she brings to the marriage, and when that amount is not enough to satisfy the husband and his family, and the bride can be killed so the husband can get a new wife with more dowry, that has to be one of the lowest valuations of a human being. Yet this is what has developed in India with the increase of capitalism and consumerism. The tradition of dowry among the wealthy was for the mother to give the bride clothing and jewelry for her wedding. But today the dowry tradition has spread to all classes of India society and thus has made the value of girls even less and of boys even more.

Although "bride burning" is outlawed, "accidents" still happen. Girls as young as eleven or twelve have been murdered in this way. Some victims survive and can relate their ordeal; I was able to talk only with women in Bombay who work to educate women regarding dowry and dowry burnings and who help families of victims both as counselor and legal representatives. There are exhibits that travel throughout India showing pictures of charred bodies alongside wedding pictures of the beautiful but demure bride.

"Some of the people in our country think the Anti-Dowry Movement is the work of the western feminist movement. They do not understand that we women here in India are doing this on our own. We appreciate the support of our sisters in other countries, but we are the ones who have to stop this practice. Most of those who oppose us are men and the women who enjoy the fruits of tradition," explained the director of the Bombay Women's Center.

MORE MYTHS THAN FACTS: RAPE

How many of these myths have you heard?

1. Women ask to be raped by the clothing they wear, or by engaging in hitchhiking and going places alone.

2. Anyone can prevent rape if they want to.

3. Rape is an impulsive act for sexual gratification.

4. Women cry "rape" to get back at a particular man or men.

5. Men who rape women are psychotic.

6. Rapists are usually minority men and their victims white women.[5]

We all have heard different figures as to the number of rapes in the United States each year. Because many rapes are not reported, the numbers vary greatly. Neither the FBI Uniform Crime Reports nor the U.S. Bureau of Justice statistics is able to draw a reliable picture because of the limited data sources. In 1990 a survey study was begun to determine more accurately the reality of rape in the United States. In their 1992 report, the National Victim Center and the Crime Victims Research and Treatment Center were able to depict the true character of rape. In their research they used the following definition for rape: "One which would be legally defined as forcible rape or criminal sexual assault in most states.

Specifically, rape was defined as 'an event that occurred without the woman's consent, involved the use of force or threat of force, and involved sexual penetration of the victim's vagina, mouth, or rectum.'[6] The study dispelled many of the myths just listed and revealed the immediate suffering and pain as well as the long-term ramifications of rape for women. A very important part of their data was the:

> clear evidence that most rapists are recidivists (offenders). A respected study of unincarcerated sex offenders provides dramatic evidence of the extent of recidivism and why it is so important for rape victims to report. Dr. Gene Able and his colleagues studied 561 unincarcreated sex offenders, of whom 126 admitted to having committed rape. *These 126 rapists had committed a total of 907 rapes involving 882 different victims. The average number of different victims per rapist is seven.*[7]

The question is, why were these 126 rapists not incarcerated? Did the women not report them? Did the police not follow up on the reports? Did the courts let them off? We do not know the answers, but we do know that if rape is not reported, the rapist remains free and able to rape again. Yet only sixteen percent, or one out of every six rapes, are ever reported to the police. Rape remains the most underreported violent crime in America.[8]

The myths for battering read as mysteriously as the myths for rape.

1. Women are basically masochistic and enjoy being battered; that's why they stay in battering situations.

2. Battering is a lower class problem.

3. Battering is directly related to alcoholism; only drunk men batter.

4. The woman provokes the beatings.

5. Men who batter are out of control.

6. "Uppity" assertive women are beaten more often than submissive women.

7. Men are battered as much as women. What about husband beating?[9]

As is true of rape, the numbers are only estimates because of very limited reporting. In states where doctors and hospitals are required to report causes of bodily injuries, many women claim various "accidents" rather than admit their husbands beat them. The National Clearinghouse for the Defense of Battered Women in their February 1994 report cites numbers ranging from one to four million women a year battered by their husbands or boyfriends. Like rape, battering is not a one-time affair. Women suffer continuous beatings during their marriages or relationships and even sometime after separation and divorce—beatings that inflict bodily injury.

Joan Zorza reports, "The injuries that battered women receive are at least as serious as injuries suffered in ninety percent of violent felony crimes, yet under state laws, they are almost always classified as misdemeanors."[10] Patrick A. Langan and Christopher A. Innes also describe the severity of injury in domestic crimes: "Victim injury is at least as common among domestic crimes that would be classified as simple assault (42%) as it is among felonies that would be classified as rape, robbery, and aggravated assault (36%). Moreover, in terms of actual bodily injury, as many as half of all incidents of domestic violence that police would classify as misdemeanors are as serious as or more serious than 90% of all the crimes that police would classify as felonies."[11]

The reporting of domestic violence is still very low. Religious convictions, economic dependency, and family pressures are often the reasons given for not reporting or for dropping the charges. Many women just want the beatings to stop, not to see their husbands or boyfriends in jail. Also, many are afraid to report because of threats to their lives or the lives of their children.

The impact on children in homes where there is domestic violence is seen in the schools and the community. When I was the teacher of emotionally disturbed children I often found in my home visits that there was violence in the home. Sometimes it was directed at both the mother and the children and sometimes only at one or the other. Often the child who suffered the physical violence was the scapegoat for the family. Wives often fill that role too.

What is even harder to detect and report is the verbal and emotional violence that women suffer. Put-downs and belittling, continual criticism, unsubstantiated accusations of infidelity, and vulgar name-calling are also forms of battering and violence to the self-esteem of the woman.

Robin Morgan paints a picture for us of the complexity of the violence against women's bodies: "The tragedy within the tragedy is that because we are regarded primarily as reproductive beings rather than full human beings, we are viewed in a (male-defined) sexual context, with the consequent epidemic of rape, sexual harassment, forced prostitution, and sexual traffic in women, with transacted marriage, institutionalized family structures, and the denial of individual women's own sexual expression."[12]

She goes on to say, "The heavy fabric suffocating women is woven so tightly from so many strands that it is impossible to examine one without encountering those intertwined with it. We can, however, summarize certain aspects of each strand, keeping in mind the interconnections—which emerge dramatically and cumulatively."[13]

There is a profile related to domestic homicide, which is the ultimate of domestic violence and battering. In their article "Who Kills Whom in Spouse Killings? On the Exceptional Sex Ratio of Spousal Homicides in the United States" in the November 1992, *Criminology*, Volume 30, M. Wilson and M. Daly identify the profile in these terms.

Men often hunt down and kill wives who have left them; women hardly ever behave similarly. Men kill wives as part of planned murders-suicides; analogous acts by women are almost unheard of. Men kill in response to revelations of wifely infidelity; women almost never respond similarly, although their mates are more often adulterous. Men often kill wives after subjecting them to lengthy periods of coercive abuse and assaults; the roles in such cases are seldom, if ever, reversed. Men perpetrate familicidal massacres, killing spouse and children together; women do not. Moreover, it seems clear that a large proportion of the spousal killings perpetrated by wives, but almost none of those perpetrated by husbands, are acts of self-defense. Unlike men, women kill male partners after years of suffering physical violence, after they have exhausted all available sources of assistance, when they feel trapped, and because they fear for their own lives.

Women the world over have suffered violence against their bodies down through the centuries. The stories that follow will help us to share some of the suffering of our sisters.

13

Female Genital Mutilation: Stories from Africa

The term female genital mutilation (FGM) is something hard for many of us, whose culture is different, even to imagine, let alone understand. After addressing a group of women in Baltimore, Maryland, when I returned from Zambia, a black woman came up to me with an angry look in her eyes. "How dare you tell stories about such barbaric acts as genital mutilation," she said. "You will have people thinking my African sisters are savages."

I am afraid that with all of her good intentions she was judging her "African sisters" by her own cultural standards. This is what we have done so often as we look at other cultures and societies. I want to make it very plain that I do not condone female genital mutilation. But before we raise our hands in horror and set our judgmental jaw square, we must understand the practice from a cultural point of view. (This goes for all cultural practices that are different from ours.) With this understanding, we can support the women within those cultures where the practice is prevalent as they work to eradicate it.

Female genital mutilation is not required by any religion. It was developed over centuries to preserve virginity, to ensure marriageability, and to suppress female sexuality—factors that are very important in many cultures. Even though it is carried out by women, it is done to preserve the girl for her husband.

THE HAND IN THE NIGHT: EGYPT

"I was six years old that night when I lay in my bed, warm and peaceful in that pleasurable state that lies half way between wakefulness and sleep, with the rosy dreams of childhood flitting by, like gentle fairies in quick succession. I felt something move under the blankets, something like a huge hand, cold and rough, fumbling over my body, as though looking for something. Almost simultaneously another hand, as cold and as rough and as big as the first one, was clapped over my mouth, to prevent me from screaming. They carried me to the bathroom."[1] Nawal el Saadawi begins her book, *The Hidden Face of Eve*, with a graphic description of her circumcision. She helps us to see both the physical pain and the psychological damage that this practice thrusts on girls for the remainder of their lives.

Saadawi gives the following description of some of the different ways that this ritual is carried out in Egypt. In one, "the procedure is extremely primitive and very much akin to Sudanese circumcision where the clitoris, external lips and internal lips are completely excised, and the orifice of the genital organs closed with a flap of sheep's intestines leaving only a very small opening barely sufficient to let the tip of the finger in, so that the menstrual and urinary flows are not held back. This opening is slit at the time of marriage and widened to allow penetration of the male sexual organ. It is widened again when a child is born. . . . Complete closure of the aperture is also done on a woman who is divorced (or widowed)."[2]

WE DIDN'T KNOW ANY DIFFERENT: KENYA

When I went to Kenya, with my son Cliff, I knew I would see Mount Kenya and hopefully some of the wild game. I was sure I would meet interesting people and enjoy renewing some friendships. What I didn't expect was what I learned from the women at Mathare Valley.

Mr. Kibatin, the social worker for the National Council of Churches of Kenya, and my son Cliff went to visit a rural/urban migration camp in Mathare Valley in Nairobi, Kenya. Ruth, one of the women leaders at the camp, came into the common room of the service building with three other women to talk with me about their lives. These women were from the northern part of Kenya, close to the Sudan border.

Ruth had a stateliness about her and seemed to be the oldest. Lois's smile lit up her face, making her look younger then her twenty years. Rachel was shy at first, keeping her eyes cast down even when she spoke. Leah, Rachel's sister, was the only one that brought a child with her. The baby slept the whole time on Leah's back.

I asked them if there was a reason that they all had English names, biblical names. "Yes," Leah said, "when we all joined the church in our village and were baptized we took Christian names. Rachel and I chose our names because we are married to the same man."

I wanted to talk to them about the difference between their traditional ways in the villages and the way things were done in the squatters' camp. I wondered if they had to give up old ways when they moved to Nairobi. I wanted to learn, but I didn't want to offend them by my questions. Ruth saved the day for me. She said, "Mr. Kibatin told me, when he asked me to bring some of my friends here to talk with you, that you were interested in knowing about our lives in the villages and here at the camp. Let me start by telling you about some of the traditions for girls and women."

As I listened, I realized what a gift I was receiving that day. They each shared stories about their lives as they grew up. Leah and Rachel told what it was like to be married to the same man. We talked and I listened as their stories opened up even more of their lives. They told of puberty rites, which were similar to the rites some of my students experienced in Zambia. Then the sparkle went out of Lois's eyes and a look of sadness and pain came over her face. I wondered what she might be remembering that was so painful. As the women talked briefly in their native language I could tell they were not all in agreement. At last Rachel shook her head and Lois turned back to speak to me. The story she told was hard for me to hear. I kept wanting to ask why they would do such a thing to her. But I remained silent and listened.

Lois began, "I want to tell you about our circumcision ritual. When I went through it I was about eleven years old. I knew about it because of my older sister Eunice. I was very afraid. I heard my mother and aunts talking one day and I knew that they were planning mine. Martha, my best friend had not gone through the ritual either. I asked her if she had heard her mother and aunts talking about it. We knew we were getting close to the age. School would be out in three days and then we would have a whole month to do what we wanted to do. Martha and I had planned to go and visit her sister who lived in a village about ten kilometers away.

"That night after all the village had gone to bed I heard something outside my sleeping hut. This whisper came in my ear, 'Lois, move over, it is Martha.' As she snuggled up next to me she told me her mother and aunts were talking after she had gone to bed. 'They are planning to have you, Naomi, Grace, and me all circumcised the first day after school is let out.'"

"'What are we going to do?' I asked. 'I remember how bad it was for Eunice. She said it felt like a hot stick going up inside of her.'

"'We must tell the other girls and make our plans for running away,' Martha said. 'Best I won't stay here tonight, we don't want our mothers to think we know what is going to happen,' Martha said as she slipped out of the hut.

"On our way to school the next day the four of us walked together. We talked about what we were going to do. We knew if we came home from school the last day our mothers and aunts would keep us so busy that we could not slip away, and it was not safe to walk through the bush at night. So we decided to tell our mothers that we wanted extra food for a party at school that day and put a dress in our book bags and on the way to school we would take the path that led to the station. Grace had a brother who worked on the train and he was always letting us ride in the baggage car with him. We decided to tell him that school had gotten out the day before and we were taking a short fun trip to one of our sisters.

"Our plans did not work. Just as we were coming around the corner of the station house there was Martha's grandmother and one of my aunts. They were on their way to the village for the ritual. All the way back her grandmother kept telling us how bad we were and my aunt kept telling us how important it was for us to have this circumcision.

"'This will make you pure and clean. This way you can be a virgin when you marry. If you don't have this, you will not be able to get married and have children,' my aunt told us.

"Grace asked her if this is what caused the baby to grow in a woman. Both of them laughed and Grace began to cry. I am not sure if she was embarrassed at them laughing at her or so afraid that crying was all she could do.

"The four of us all slept together that night in a special hut that had been built out to the edge of the village that day. It wasn't a real hut. There was no roof, just a round enclosure made of branches with an opening for a door that had a cloth hung over it. Our uncles stayed outside all night to make sure that we did not try to get away again. We did not do much sleeping. All we could think about was what was going to happen the next day.

"Just as the eastern sky was turning grey Naomi's mother brought in some tea for us. That is all we got for breakfast. She said they did not want us to have a lot to eat so we would not get sick.

"By this time we were so afraid and tired that nothing else could scare us. We each put our *chtangy*[3]—two meters of cloth—around us and sipped our tea. None of us spoke. When we had finished, my sister Eunice came in and tried to comfort us. This time she was telling us that it really didn't hurt that much and when it was over we would be women. I thought, I don't want to be a woman, I want to play and go to school and learn. I don't want to have children, not now.

"We could hear voices. As they got louder, the closer the four of us got. By the time our mothers, aunts, grandmothers, and older sisters pulled back the cloth over the door we were holding each other in a close knot.

"As the women walked in they were singing a chant about how women must be pure for their husbands and how they are to serve their husbands and never serve another man. The grandmothers, both our father's mother and our mother's mother, came to each of us. The aunts had laid four special mats, in a cross shape. We each were told to lay down on our backs. We knew we could not yell out because you never heard a sound coming from the circumcision hut. Our sisters put a piece of cloth in our mouths and held our heads between their knees as they knelt on the ground above our heads. Our mothers and aunts held our legs and arms while our grandmothers cut us. I was so afraid that I kept my eyes closed once they had taken a hold of my arms and legs.

"The singing stopped and all you could hear were the drums beating. I could tell it was for dancing. I wanted to be out there dancing but I knew I would have to stay in the hut for at least a week. Sometimes girls had to stay in the hut for the whole month.

"After the hot sizzling pain I felt something warm running down my leg and under my hips—the next thing I knew I was laying with my head in my sister's lap and felt very sick all over. I looked up at her and asked her how she and mother could let them do this to me. Then I yelled at her to get out. I didn't want to ever see her again. I yelled so hard that I felt something warm between my legs where the pain was the greatest. My sister jumped up and ran out calling mother that I was bleeding again. I was not able to go back to school by the end of the month because I had not healed right and they had to take me to the hospital. Because of the infection I will never be able to have children the doctors say. My grandmother does not believe them, but I have not been able to get married because of my circumcision."

I was so moved by her story I just sat there for a few moments. Then Rachel spoke. She had been quiet behind her shy face. "I think you should know that when the missionaries came to our village they tried to teach the women about health and their bodies, but it was many years before some of the mothers started questioning why girls had to be circumcised. Most of us have had problems because of it. If not infections and illnesses, many of us are afraid even to have our husbands touch us between the legs. Because of the pain we did not always keep ourselves as clean as we should."

I wanted to ask if they had any sense of pleasure when they had intercourse with their husbands, but was not sure just how they might respond. Leah helped me out.

"I did not know until I came to Nairobi and read some magazines that women are supposed to get pleasure out of sex. That we are to enjoy it and want it. I knew I never had, and so I asked a woman doctor from Germany, who was working here at the clinic, about what it meant when it said women enjoyed sex. How could that be? We have to be cut open for our wedding night. It is always painful to have intercourse. So painful that we don't even want to have it.

"I will never let any one cut on me again. When my first husband died a year after we were married, the women of the village wanted to sew me back up. That is when I said, 'No!' My grandfather, the head clansman, told me I had to or to leave. I left. A few months later he came to the station town where I was living and working at the mission school and asked me to come home."

Now they wanted to ask me some questions. "Peggy, do you women have to have these kinds of rituals for you to become a woman?" asked Rachel.

"No," I said trying to imagine what it must be like.

Lois, the adventurous one, had a questioning sparkle in her eyes when she asked me, "What is the pleasure like when you have sex? What does it mean that you enjoy it? Is it like when you see your best friend and give each other a hug?"

How was I going to explain how women can enjoy their sexuality to women who have had children but never experienced the wonders of an orgasm? "Do you remember the joy you felt when you gave birth to your first child and you held it?" I asked.

"I was so happy. I cried. I laughed. I felt like I wanted to shout and sing. I have never been so happy." There was a moment of silence then Leah continued, "Do you mean that is what you feel when you enjoy sex?"

"That is one way of explaining it."

The women were very still, then the expression on their faces became angry and determined. Ruth's eyes looked as if they could set the place on fire. "You mean we have suffered all our lives, from fear as children that we would have to be circumcised, and from the pain, both in our bodies and in our heads, because we were circumcised. Now you tell us that there is pleasure and enjoyment in having sex for women also. The nurses and doctors have been telling us circumcision is bad for our health and for our children's health. Some women have real trouble at childbirth because of it. I am not going to allow my daughters to go through it. We have got to do something to stop this. We women don't need to be physically protected so we can serve our husbands."

The women were all talking at the same time now. I could not tell what they were saying, but I could tell they were angry. Their voices were getting louder and louder when Mr. Kibatin and Cliff came through the door. "What's happening here?" Mr. Kibatin asked.

They stopped and looked up in surprise. Ruth spoke, "We have a couple more questions to ask Peggy; could you two leave until we are finished?"

With a startled look the two men turned and left. All eight eyes looked intently at me as Ruth said, "We want to know, is there some way that we can learn to enjoy sex?"[4]

"I don't know," I answered. "I guess you could learn about enjoying the touching of other parts of your body. You could learn about your own sexuality and how to enjoy it. I am not sure where you could find help in that way. You will need to talk with a doctor to learn if there is anything that can be done about the circumcision."

"We have been talking about these things," said Lois, "but we don't have a woman doctor here anymore, and the only women here are African women and I don't think they know that much about enjoying sex. Not like you American women."

"I hope you don't have the idea that American women do nothing but have sex," I said. "Most of us are monogamous and have a relationship with only one man at a time. Some of our magazines and TV shows and movies would lead you to think that all we do is go to bed with men. But most of us do enjoy sexual relationships with men," I added.

They each gave me a big hug and we walked out the door laughing.

14

Children Are Becoming the Choice of Men: Stories from Asia

WE HAD TO SELL OUR DAUGHTERS: THAILAND

"We had to sell our daughter so we could feed the family." "A trader kidnapped our daughter and we don't know where she is." "Our daughter was enticed away with the promise of money, pretty clothes, and living in Bangkok." These are some of the comments I heard when I talked to families in the villages close to Chiang Mai.

Although country after country after country is passing legislation against child prostitution, the business is growing.[1]

"Prostitution is an integrated social pathology and the prevalence of child prostitution lays bare the fundamental attitudes inherent in Western society, the rotten moral core of a world view based on affluence as the primary criteria," stated Professor Prawase Wasi of the faculty of medicine at Mahidol University, Siriraj Hospital, Bangkok, Thailand, in his keynote address at the consultation on *Caught In Modern Slavery: Tourism and Child Prostitution in Asia*, held in Chiang Mai, Thailand, May 1-5, 1990.[2]

Professor Wasi also discussed the linkage between economic deterioration of the less-developed countries and the power and influence of the industrial countries on all levels of government in the poorer countries. He showed how the many different social problems—rural poverty, crimes, violence, wars, and destruction of the environment—come from the same root causes.

"Groups who work on local development projects, peace, non-violence, education, and environment are addressing the same common issues and should combine forces. For example, ecological agriculture is an integrated approach which should be promoted. It can achieve most purposes in an integrated way. It is a sustainable economic system for farmers. It nourishes the environment. It keeps community life intact. It is a 'spiritual' livelihood that helps people to bring needed fulfillment to their lives. Integrated farming will lessen the tragic pressures on farmers which inevitably include the option of selling their children into prostitution," Professor Wasi summarizes.[3]

On March 31, 1993, full-page ads were placed in all major Asian newspapers by the global End Child Prostitution in Asian Tourism (ECPAT) Network, a coalition of more than 200 child advocacy agencies, church groups, and development agencies in twenty-three countries. Some of the points made in the ad were:

- More than one million children are forced into prostitution every year, living in conditions akin to slavery. Most of them are living in Asia.

- Recent years have seen a shocking increase in the number of prostituted children.

- Some countries have over 100,000 children in prostitution, but still there are not enough to meet the demand.

- Child-trafficking across the borders between many Asian countries is an increasingly serious problem.

- Why this demand?

- Too many tourists exploit the poverty of local people by demanding children for prostitution.

- Some mistakenly believe they will be safe from AIDS if they have sex with children.[4]

Young girls are trapped in prostitution from the Amazon region of Brazil, to the cities of Africa, to the brothels of Asia, and even in the industrial nations. In their October 1993 newsletter, ECPAT-USA—West lists these numbers of child prostitution in Asian countries:

- PAKISTAN, at least 200,000 Bengali women prostitutes, 20 percent are children.

- INDIA, 1,500,000–2,000,000 prostitutes, 20 percent under age 16 (300,000–4000,000 children).

- NEPAL, 150,000 girls in Indian brothels, 20 percent or more under age.

- CHINA, total unknown, estimated 5,000 in Sichaun province alone.

- TAIWAN, at least 100,000 child prostitutes.

- THAILAND, 200,000–300,000 children.

- VIETNAM, 40,000 children (government estimate).

- PHILIPPINES, 1,200,000 street children. Number of prostituted children not known, estimate over 100,000.

Helping young girls escape their dangerous environment, continue their education, and learn new life skills is often a very isolated work carried out by many different kinds of organizations, usually staffed by women. Their voices have not typically been heard in cities or rural villages, nor on the national or international level. Their expertise in this social problem is not recognized or sought out.[5]

The issues surrounding prostitution and child prostitution are many and varied. The story of the work against prostitution in Bangkok and the stories of the mothers in the villages outside of Chiang Mai reflect the complex web that is enslaving women.

Thailand Is Beautiful, But Not Everything Is Beautiful

Spring is a beautiful time of the year in Bangkok. But I soon learned that not all is beautiful in Bangkok. My hostess, Boonmee Julkiree of the women's department of the Church of Christ of Thailand, had picked me up to go to the International Christian Church for the preview of the film *Tomorrow Will There Be a Rainbow?* on child prostitution. Again my horizons were stretched beyond anything I could have imagined. It was Holy Week, with services commemorating suffering and death, but they also gave the hope of resurrection. Was there any hope for these children?

Professor Rutnin Mattani of Thammasat University's drama department had produced the film. She related to me what led to her making it: "When I saw in the papers about the fire that destroyed a brothel at Phuket Island and five young girls whose ages ranged from nine to twelve burning alive, I decided to do something about child prostitution."

The film showed the intensity of the flames and then the unrecognizably charred bodies of the five small girls with arms that resembled burnt sticks and stiffened hands reaching out for help. The basement ruins, where the girls had been locked in a room, was all that was left of the brothel. The scene moved to the northern part of Thailand—the districts of Lampoon, Chiang Rai, Payao, and Chiang Mai, where I was going the following week. This is the area where most of the young girls come from who ended up in the teahouses of Bangkok and the brothels of the tourist resorts.[6]

The film was the beginning of my education about this slave trade called prostitution. Boonmee then took me to the Bangkok Emergency Home, where I met Khunying Kanitha Wichiencharoen, the director. The home works to provide different kinds of rehabilitation for the young girls. Police bring some of the girls arrested in raids to the home to help them become rehabilitated and others are found in the Patpong Street red-light district by social workers and volunteer women. That spring alone, the Bangkok police had picked up more than one hundred young girls, thirteen and fourteen years old. About ten percent of all prostitutes are under fourteen years of age.

The next week I flew to Chiang Mai.

Under the Ceiba Tree

The emerald green of the fields and the colorful dress of the people made a kaleidoscope of the countryside. Mark picked me up at the guest house of the seminary where I stayed the first two days of my time in Chiang Mai. Mark was a high school classmate of mine. Every since I first knew he was in Thailand I had thought it be wonderful to visit him someday. That someday took many years to come but here I was.

We climbed on his motorcycle. My backpack on, my arms around his waist, the wind in my face, we headed for his home in a village outside of Chiang Mai. What a wonderful way to see the countryside!

Susan, Mark's wife, came out of the house when she heard the roar of the cycle. Here is where I would begin to experience rural Thai life with all its joys and sorrows, pain and hope.

The next three mornings, Susan and I climbed on her motorcycle and headed to different villages to meet with the women. It was kapok-stripping time.[7] The women might be sitting under a tree or under their houses. Some houses were built up on stilts, and the space underneath was used for many different activities.

The first morning we sat under a huge tree that reminded me of the flame trees in Zambia with their wide-spreading limbs. Women sat around a cloth spread out in the middle. Each woman had a pile of pods and a small bowl and a larger basket placed beside her. Most of the pods were already cracked open, so we only had to pull them apart, strip out the kapok, and pull out the seeds. We threw the kapok in the middle, put the seeds in the bowl, and the pods in the basket to be carried to the pigs later for feed.

The women knew we were coming and they had saved a place for us to sit. The talking quieted as we took our places by the woman at whose home we had gathered. With Susan's help I soon learned that they had been talking about their rice crop and how they were not going to be able to sell it if they could not get transportation. As I listened, I learned how these women planned and worked together. It wasn't until the second day, in another village, as we again sat and stripped kapok pods that I began to hear about daughters who had been sold by their fathers or kidnapped by traders and taken to Bangkok as child prostitutes. Here were the mothers, aunts, and older sisters of some of the children I had heard about the week before in Bangkok.

I quietly explained to Susan about seeing the film and the places that Boonmee had taken me. I asked her if she could help me learn about why their girls were now in Bangkok. One of the mothers told Susan she would tell me her story.

"We are very poor people. We cannot sell our rice[8] and so we only have kapok and some crafts that we can sell to get money. We have a very large family: six sons and four daughters. We cannot feed all of them. My husband had a chance to sell our ten-year-old daughter to a trader for 20,000 Baht (U.S. $800), more money then we would get in two years from our rice if we could sell it. I didn't want him to sell her. She was so young. But what could we do? We could not feed the other children. I cried the night the trader came and got her. She did not know what was happening. We did not tell her. We can't read or write so I cannot write to her. I do not know where she is or how she is. The trader told me she would be well taken care of but I do not believe him. I have another daughter who will be ten this fall. Already my husband is trying to sell her also. We have been told that it is against the law, but what are we to do?"

The woman's voice was sometimes so soft I wondered how Susan could hear what she was saying. There were times when the mother had to stop and wipe her eyes before she could go on with her story. When she had finished we all sat and worked in silence for a while. The only sound was from the pods as they lit in the baskets. My heart was pounding and I had a pain in my gut. I wondered if any of the girls I had seen at the Bangkok Emergency Home had been her daughter or if she was still at a teahouse or locked away in a brothel. I too had to wipe tears from my eyes.

Our host for the day turned and spoke to me, "I see you also weep for our girls and our families. Do you have daughters that might be used this way?"

Susan told her I had only three sons, but that I had visited a home in Bangkok that was trying to help the young girls.

I asked Susan to tell them, "My tears are because I am a mother also and know that losing a child is very painful. My tears are for you, the mothers."

Some women told me stories about their daughters being kidnapped or being enticed away with the chance for money and pretty clothes. I also learned of the hopes that the mothers had in trying to improve their economic situation so they would not have to sell their daughters to feed the other children. They were also learning about family planning and child spacing.

During my last evening with Mark and Susan we talked about all of the factors that played into child prostitution. They told me about the poverty of the farmers, their lack of schooling, some of the social and cultural practices, and the sex tourism. Businessmen from the industrial nations—Japan, Germany, United States, and Australia—come to Thailand just for that purpose. They also told me that during the Chinese New Year, Chinese men come to Thailand to have sex with girls who have not yet reached puberty, because they think it will increase or restore their virility.

BRIDES ARE BEAUTIFUL AND BURNED: INDIA

Traditions die hard in most cultures. Values that are passed down from generation to generation will change only when those who are in an adversary position seek to change them. This is what the Anti-Dowry Movement in India is seeking to do.

The tradition of dowry has changed in recent years. Historically it was part of the wealthy class tradition of providing clothes and jewelry for the bride and some household articles. How has this changed and why?

The modernization of India after its independence in 1947 brought about a consumer culture that engulfed the entire country. Thus, the tradition of dowry has taken on the elements of consumerism. Men in all economic classes now expect to be given a dowry when taking a bride. This has led to hardships for poor families and an increase in the death rate of female children. Female infanticide has been outlawed, but the female infant mortality rate is now thirty to sixty percent higher than that of male children.[9]

While I was in Bombay, I visited with the director of the Bombay Women's Center. She told me stories of women who were murdered because they did not take enough dowry with them at the time of their marriage or were not able to provide extra items that the in-laws demanded. For one young bride, whose father was a scooter driver, the mother-in-law kept asking the bride's father for more. She threatened him with his daughter having "an accident" if he did not give them a TV and another 1,000 rupees. The accident—a fire—happened, but the daughter was able to run from the house and quench her burning clothes by rolling in the water in the gutter. She lived for four days and was able to tell her mother what had happened. Yet when the police asked her if her husband or any of her in-laws had set her on fire she said, "No." The director said, "Many women think they cannot say anything against their husbands to the authorities."

Much of this goes back to Hindu Manu scripture teachings that a daughter must obey her father; a wife, her husband; a widow, her sons. The Anti-Dowry Movement is attacking bride-burning on many fronts. Movement leaders realize that laws will not change traditions. They are working toward educating women about their rights. They are organizing women to stand together against dowry exchange, helping women to see that the dowry is a method of being bought and sold. They are investigating deaths and bringing husbands and in-laws into court. And they are providing support and counseling for families of the brides.

As Elisabeth Bumiller writes in her book, *May You Be the Mother of a Hundred Sons: A Journey Among the Women of India*, it is very hard to find a survivor of a bride-burning. I was not able to talk with one, but after listening to the center's director and reading about bride-burning I wonder how one woman, a mother-in-law, could do this kind of violence to another woman—or to any person.

15

Men's Honor—Women's Lives: Stories from Latin America

TO KILL FOR HONOR: MEXICO

It was a beautiful warm day in the city of eternal spring, Cuernavaca, Mexico. A group of us, with our male and female guides were going to a village to talk with a rural health worker about health needs in that part of Mexico. As we approached the small whitewashed adobe building, with the doors and windows painted bright blue, we were not prepared for what we found inside. Juanita was the rural health worker in her village. She had been selected by the community for special training in first aid and herbal medicine. Her mother had been the herbal woman and Juanita had learned about caring for the villagers from her. We were looking forward to learning about how she gathered, dried, and prepared her medicines. Instead we learned about a different part of their culture.

As we entered the small room, we saw Alicia sitting in the corner putting dried herbs on pieces of paper and folding them up for the people who would need them. Alicia was not able to talk because her mouth was swollen shut. Her husband Carlos had hit her and broken her jaw. Her friend Juanita, in whose home she was staying, told us her story. (Cindy, one of our guides, suggested that Kirk, the other guide, take the men over to the house across the street where some of the village men had gathered.)

Alicia and Carlos had been married for a little over a year when Carlos began accusing Alicia of being unfaithful. Alicia's cousin José, whom she was raised with, had moved to another part of Mexico when he was fourteen to live with an aunt on his father's side of the family. Now he had moved back to work the small parcel of land that had been his father's. Alicia spent time with José and often cooked for him because he was not married and had no one to care for him. They were more like brother and sister than cousins. Carlos knew this because he had grown up with both Alicia and José. In fact, Carlos and José had been the best of friends when they were boys. Yet Carlos was very jealous.

Juanita told us what had happened. "One day last week Carlos came home and found José eating his supper and sitting in the chair that Carlos always sat in. He yelled at José to get out of his house and to never come back again.

"José left, but he told me later he did not know why Carlos was so angry at him," Juanita explained.

"It was after José left and Carlos could see that he was headed down the road that he turned to Alicia and in a rage started to hit her with the hot tortilla pan. She was able to protect her head with her arms until he grabbed one of them, and that is when he hit her on the side of the head and broke her jaw. It also knocked her out. Carlos thought she was dead. He went to his brother Jorge and told him he had killed Alicia for honor," Juanita said.

"Just what does that mean? I have heard of it but I don't understand," I asked.

"Men think that they have the right to kill their wives if they think they are being unfaithful to them. It is all part of the machismo that men seem to think they have to have. If women even thought of killing for honor, because their husbands were sleeping around, there wouldn't be any husbands left," Juanita laughed. "Men think that women are to be faithful to them but they don't have to be faithful to their wives."

"Let me make sure I understand this. A husband can kill his wife if she is sleeping around or he even thinks she is. Aren't there any laws about this?" I asked.

"If a man kills his wife he can claim honor and usually get off completely or with a very light sentence. But if a woman kills her husband because he is beating up on her and/or the kids, she is usually convicted." Juanita said.

"What happened to Carlos? Where is he now?" I asked.

"He is at his house, but he comes here every day trying to get Alicia to come back home. I will not let Alicia talk with him. Last night he broke into my house and tried to kidnap her. She yelled, the best she could with her broken jaw, and I was ready to hit him with this stick." Juanita held up a stick at least the size of a baseball bat. "With my help Alicia told him she was not going to come home. She did not trust him. If he could think that there was something going on between her and José then he was out of his mind and she did not trust him not to hit her again."

All the time Juanita was talking Alicia was shaking her head in agreement. I could see the anger behind her tears. Alicia had not known that Carlos was so jealous of other men until José had come home. Alicia had been faithful and the other men in the community knew that Alicia loved Carlos very much. She had loved him ever since they were children playing together—Carlos, José, Alicia, and Juanita. Alicia had seen her father hit her mother when her father got drunk, but she had never seen him jealous. So when Carlos began accusing Alicia of seeing José, she did not know what to think. She tried to remind Carlos that José was like a brother to her and was his best friend, but Carlos would get even more angry. He had hit Alicia with his hand before but nothing like this. Juanita said that Alicia would have stayed with Carlos if he had not gone around bragging about killing her for his honor. She realized that he would continue bragging, even if José never came by the house again. But how could she not let her brother come to her home?

I asked Juanita if this was a common happening in the village. She told me that men think they have the right to do whatever they want to their women—wives, daughters, mistresses. "We in the Basic Christian Community (BCC) have talked about how Jesus treated women," she continued. "We women have formed our own Bible study group to help us find ways to help our menfolk to understand they are not to hit us and how we can change things for ourselves."

While we were there, Carlos came to the door again, this time very quiet and almost subdued. He asked again to see Alicia and Juanita told him, "No!" She reminded him that Alicia could not talk because he had broken her jaw and it was swollen shut by this time. When Carlos saw us there was fire in his eyes.

"Are you telling them about what happened?" he yelled as he pointed his finger at us. "You women are all alike. You tell each other lies. All lies. Alicia and José were sleeping together. You just don't understand. We men have to be macho." Carlos continued to yell.

I got up and walked toward him. "I would like to hear your side of what happened," I said. "I would like to learn more about why macho and machismo are so very important to you. I want to understand more about honor."

"No, you are just trying to trick me. I don't trust you or any woman!" he shouted as he turned to leave. Mark, one of the men in our group, had remained just outside the door. He overheard Carlos yelling and followed him to the neighbor's house, where the other men of our group were. Carlos began drinking beer and ranting about why he had to defend his honor.

WHAT IS THIS HONOR?

After we left the village Mark told us his experience. He said he talked with young men in their early twenties, one teenage boy, several men in their thirties, and two elders of the village. This is how he understood honor, macho, and machismo from the men.

The man is the king in his castle—"*en mi casa yo mando*" (in my house, I command)—which is the supreme role of the husband. All must accept his authority. He has the right to do what ever he chooses within his house. He has been brought up this way. He is taught in the home to be macho. This includes, along with having sexual prowess, to be physically strong, to be adventurous and have courage, and to defend the honor of the family, both that of his parents' family and his own when he has one. This also includes the extended family.

In defending the honor of the family, the sons are responsible for looking after their sisters, both older and younger. Young males have a lot more freedom of movement. They are not questioned when they come in late at night or even if they stay out all night. Any behavior that enhances their manliness, their machismo, is acceptable. Therefore fights, drinking, and defending the family honor are looked on as appropriate activities. Even though they have to defend the honor of their own sisters, apparently they are free to try to dishonor other girls who are not part of their family. This is where some of the fighting comes in. If a boy shows some attention to a girl and the brother does not like the boy or thinks he is wanting to dishonor the girl, the brother will defend his sister, even if there is no reason for his actions.

Although the male has freedom of movement, there are social restraints on him. He must not do anything that will prevent him from caring for his wife and children. If he can afford it, it is acceptable for him to have a mistress, but most of the men prove their machismo by buying liquor and women. His carousing tells the other men that he is so much a man that his wife cannot satisfy him. If his sexual promiscuity or his drinking affects his ability to provide for his family, both the community and the in-laws will question him on his behavior. If his extramarital adventures become blatant, his reputation in the community may be damaged and bring dishonor to his parents. These are the only restraints on his conduct.

If he suspects his wife of sexual promiscuity—a heinous crime—a husband has a right to defend his honor. If he feels his wife has brought this on and is a willing party, he will either abandon her—for to live with a promiscuous wife is not honorable—or he will kill her to save his honor. One indiscretion by a wife and she pays either with her life or with rejection by the husband and her own family, which has also been dishonored.

Mark said that one of the elders told him that women suffer very much because of machismo.

SLOW BUT SURE: CHANGE

The next day my friends Betty and Anna and I went to a Cuernavaca BCC women's group that we had been meeting with twice a week for five weeks. There were four women in the group that day besides the three of us. Eight women belonged but the most that had ever been there were five. Maria was the oldest. She had four children, two of whom were married. She also had three grandchildren. Maria was a natural leader, although the group did not have a formal structure. Luz was the youngest. She was Maria's daughter and had just finished public school. She hoped to study to be a teacher. She did not have a boyfriend because they had broken up. She said she was not going to date until she finished school. "Boys want all of your attention. I can't study and have a boyfriend," she said.

Rosa had been married the year before and was now four months pregnant. She had gone to college one year and then had gotten married. She agreed with Luz that you can't study if you have a boyfriend. "Men, they take all your time. My husband would be very mad if he knew what we talk about here," she said.

The fourth woman was very quiet and shy. I wondered if it was because of the black eye she had and the cut on her arm where the blood showed through the bandage. Her name was Paula.

Because the previous day's experience was still so fresh in our minds, we asked the women to tell us their feelings about their relationships with their husbands, machismo, and how it affected their lives.

Betty asked, "Rosa, why would your husband be mad if he knew what we talked about here?" Rosa's remark had surprised the three of us. We didn't think we were talking about anything that would be disruptive to the families or the community. The women talked about their problems: how to get clean water, or books for the school children, or pavement on the street, or the garbage hauled off on a regular bases.

"My husband thinks that when women talk they create problems. He thinks I would get wrong ideas here," she said.

"What kind of wrong ideas?" I inquired.

"He says that women's talk makes a wife disrespectful to her husband," Rosa answered.

"My husband questions me also every time I come to one of these meetings," said Paula. "He wants to know what we talk about. I tell him we study the Bible and we talk about how to get books for our children's schools. He doesn't mind my studying the Bible, but he tells me that it is the menfolk that are to take care of things outside the home."

I wondered if he gave her the black eye and cut her because he didn't like her coming to these meetings. Maybe she isn't as shy as I thought. Maybe she is standing up to her husband.

"You said that you talked with a woman yesterday whose husband had tried to kill her because of his honor," Rosa stated. "Machismo and honor seem to get mixed up in most men's minds. They think that it is macho to carouse around. They don't think about the honor of the wife or how she feels, knowing her husband is sleeping with other women. I know some people say we women accept that as part of our culture. Let me tell you many of us do not accept it. Not any more."

"Many of us have shut the door and thrown away the key. We don't let them back in the house. I kicked my husband out after my fourth daughter was born," Maria said. "He said I was a lousy wife and that I must be sleeping around because he was sure he could have a son. He told me his mistress had a son by him. I asked him how he was sure it was his son. If she slept with him she is probably sleeping with other men." When Maria got wound up her eyes shot fire.

Luz spoke, "I can remember Papa coming by and harassing Mama. One time he tried to take my oldest sister with him. But Mama had told us where and how to hit a man who tried to do things to us that we didn't want them to do. My sister hit Papa and he struggled off all doubled up. That was the last time he tried to take any of us with him. We knew what he wanted us to do. He needed money because he had lost his job when Mama kicked him out. He thought that if he had one of us girls to sell for prostitution he would have money for his beer. His mistress had left him when he could no longer buy her pretty clothes." Luz was a fireball just like her Mama.

"One of the things that we women have begun to do is to stand together and support each other when our husbands beat us or will not give us money for the family," Maria said.

"When my husband hit me and cut me the other night after he came home drunk, I was able to get my baby and run out of the house," Paula said. "I knew I couldn't go to my family. They would just say, 'You are his wife, that is his child. He has a right to do what ever he wants to you in his home.' I came over here to Maria's knowing we would be safe here."

Maria's was the safe house. There was no man there and now that two of her children were gone she had room for other women. "I guess you would say I am the mother hen. I take in all the battered women in the *colonia*."[1]

Anna asked, "Are there other ways that you have worked together in trying to stop the abuse of women and children?"

Luz was ready with an answer. "We have gotten the priest to preach about how God created us all equal. I remember when he preached on the story in Genesis Chapter 1, one of the men after church asked the priest, 'What happened to Adam's rib? I thought that is where woman came from. I thought woman came from Adam.' Then one time he preached about how we are all equal. Something about Greeks and Jews, male and female, slave and free. It was after these sermons that the men began complaining that the priest was listening to the women too much. It was over this that my boyfriend and I broke up. He didn't believe the things the priest was saying were in the Bible. I tried to show him, but he would not listen. He told me that when we got married I had to do everything he told me to do. He should have known better than to say that to me. I told him he could have his bracelet back.[2] No man was going to tell me what to do."

Rosa told us about how she was helping one of the nuns to write some Bible study materials for husbands and wives. "We hope to get our husbands to come to these Bible studies and see how it is that Jesus wants families to live. We know it will take a long time to change the way most of the men think, but if we could get some of the men to change, maybe they could help others to respect their wives."

CONCLUSION

We find that most cultures honor machismo and macho behavior. It takes on different forms and is called by different names. We see women suffer greatly regardless of what it is called. In Latin American society, it is clearly named and is socially accepted. An honor killing in Mexico carries a different banner of acceptance than does a bride-burning in India. Yet women are saying "enough is enough." There are Marias and Paulas in every community who have stood up to their husbands and said, "No more."

As women come together either informally, as in the group above, or formally, as in battered women's shelters and rape-crisis centers, they find support in a safe environment. They learn, as printed on a bumper sticker, that only "Men Can Stop The Rapes." They have come to know also that only through their own empowerment and the education of men will the lifestyles of men change.

16

Home and Work—Violence Is There: Stories from the United States

When I started to prepare for this chapter, a chapter I knew I had to write, I had no idea how powerfully it would affect me. I was raped in 1981. I sought rape-crisis counseling and the support of my extended family. Some years later I told my three sons about it, but I did not go public for ten years. It can take a long time before a woman can talk about rape outside of counseling sessions or with trusted friends. If tears come from the stories I will be sharing, just know that those tears are in the company of mine and many other sisters. The names of the people have all been changed, as have the locations, because some of us are still living in fear.

SHE SHOULD HAVE BEEN ABLE TO TRUST HIM

Clara was a middle-aged woman whose zest for life concealed her age. She was an attractive widow who had gone back to work after her husband was killed in a car accident. She was well liked in her office and was always there with a willing hand to help out. She still had a son at home and a daughter in college. Her friends were happy for her because she was now getting out after a year of wondering what she was going to do. The small midwestern city had been her home for the twenty years of her marriage.

Her best friend at work, May, had the desk next to Clara's. Friday evenings May and Clara and two other women always stopped at a small restaurant for a glass of wine and a light supper. Her son, Carl, had supper at his girlfriend Beth's house and then they would go to the game; Carl played football and Beth was a cheerleader.

Once in awhile some of the men from the office would stop by the same restaurant. This particular Friday night Clara's car was in the shop getting repaired.

As the women were finishing their meal, Bruce, a salesman for the company, and Larry, the district manager, came in. Larry bought them all a round of wine and then Clara told them she had to leave and catch the bus home before it stopped running.

"I live out your way. I'll drop you off," said Bruce.

Clara wondered how he knew where she lived, because he had only been working for the company about six weeks. He had moved from Chicago. It was beginning to get a little nippy out with the fall winds announcing winter was not far behind, so Clara accepted Bruce's offer. Now she would not have to walk the two blocks home from the bus stop. May waved good-bye as she teased Clara, "Don't yell so much at the game tonight that you lose your voice again."

The next Monday morning everyone seemed to be in a great mood and May was talking about her weekend out of town. "May, can you come into my office?" Larry asked urgently.

The look on his face told May that something had happened. She had known Larry since high school days. They could read each other almost like husband and wife. "What is it Larry? What has happened?" she asked fearfully.

"It's Clara, she was found out on River Road last Friday night about nine o'clock. She was wandering around and badly beaten up. She's in the hospital. Carl just called me to say that his mother would not be in to work."

"I am going over now," May said.

"Let's go together. I want to know how she got out on River Road. Didn't she leave the restaurant with Bruce last Friday night?" Larry said.

Clara's jaw was wired shut and both eyes were bandaged. The doctors were not sure how badly her eyes were injured. There were also broken bones and internal injuries that required surgery. She had just been taken off the critical list but was still in intensive care.

Carl was sitting in the waiting room with Beth and her mother.

"Carl, did she tell you who did this do her?" May asked.

"All she said to the couple that found her was 'Bruce, Bruce.' The doctors say she was in a state of shock when they found her and she still has not come out of it."

"May, do you know a Bruce?" Carl asked. His eyes were sad yet there was a fire that burned in them.

"Yes. There is a Bruce at work. In fact he gave your mother a ride home on Friday evening. They left the restaurant around six-thirty," Larry said. "May, you stay here, I am going back to the office and find Bruce."

Neither Larry nor the police was able to find Bruce. The manager of his apartment said she had not seen him for over a week. He had skipped town. Clara went for rape-crisis counseling when she got out of the hospital.

May told me Clara's story when I went to visit her, and we talked about violence against women. May asked me about my rape and I told her my story.

MINISTERS ARE NOT NECESSARILY ANGELS

The first time that Tom sexually assaulted me, I was so shocked that all I could do was yell "No!" and run out of the office. I was standing in his office facing the bookshelves looking for books that might help me in preparing for the sermon I had been invited to preach in a couple of weeks. I heard someone come in but did not look around. Then I felt him up against me, his arms reaching around me, and his hands on my breasts. I am not sure where I got the strength to push his arms away. He is over six feet tall and weighs well over two hundred pounds. I ran out of the church and got into my car and drove and drove and drove. Driving is very therapeutic for me.

I am not sure why I was so shocked. He had been telling me if I was lonely he could help me relieve my loneliness. He also talked about us going to another city about 150 miles away for an overnighter. I had told him I did not need his help and that I did not like being talked to that way. He gave me his little laugh and said, "All women like sexy talk, that's how you get your jollies." He also was always saying that he would deny that he ever said or did anything that I might say he had done, unless of course it made him look good.

The next morning I did not go into the church until I was sure the secretary would be there. She and I shared the same office. When Tom came in I told him I needed to talk with him right then and that it was important. He tried to make excuses but I was assertive and followed him into his office. As he began to close the door I said, "Leave it open." Then looking him straight in the eye I told him, "Don't you ever touch me again." I turned and walked out of the office and went to the room where I was setting up a nursery school for the church. There was an intercom there, I called the secretary and told her I was leaving it on so she could hear what I was doing and saying in the room.

Tom did not touch me again and things stayed on a very formal business level between us. The secretary asked me after a week of having the intercom on if something was wrong. "You don't seem your usual happy sparkling self." Even Paul, the man I was building the playground with, asked me, "Is something wrong? Did I say something to offend you, Peggy?"

Two weeks passed. It was a hot May day and the air conditioner had not been turned on yet. When I finished my brown-bag lunch I decided to lie down on the carpet in Tom's office where it was cooler to rest a while. Tom had left that morning and said he would be out for the day. I hadn't been resting long when I felt a body against me and heard a zipping sound. I rolled over and jumped up and there lay Tom half exposed. I left the church and went to the home where I was staying while I was on this short-term appointment. I called my friends in Tucson, Arizona, to see if I could go to see them. I was planning to leave that August for Zambia and was trying to visit all of my friends before I left. I flew to Arizona the next day.

The love and support I found there with my friends gave me the courage to take action. When I returned I tried to contact the head of the church for that region, but he was on vacation. I had one week left to finish what I had come to do. I told myself I can finish and then leave. Even though I knew I was not at fault, I was still feeling embarrassed. I was in a strange town. I did not know anyone when I went there. There was no one I could talk to because Tom was a "pillar" of the community.

The first day I was back was Tom's day off. The next day when I went to the room to work, I locked myself in and left on the intercom. Of course Tom had keys to all the rooms but at least he could not just slip in. I left the room to get some materials out of my car. When I returned and opened the door, the room was dark. As I reached to turn on the light Tom grabbed me and threw me on the mattresses he had taken out of the baby cribs. I screamed and yelled. He put one hand over my mouth and pulled my pants down with his other hand. I was able to flip myself over and started kicking him in the back. Then he hit me so hard I was dazed. I knew then that he would beat me up if I did not stop fighting him.

When he finished raping me, he went into the children's bathroom that was part of the nursery school. I was unable to move. As he walked out the door he said, "That will teach you to tell me, NO."

I struggled to get to my car. After driving around for about an hour I went to another minister, Ed, to tell him what had happened. Tom was already there. He had told Ed that I was making sexual advances toward him and that he wanted me to leave. I told Ed that Tom had raped me. Ed did not believe me and said that if I pressed charges Tom could sue me for libel. I should also think about Tom's wife and children. I knew then that I would have no support from the clergy in that town. I also knew that the police would not listen to me, because Tom's brother was the chief of police. We agreed that I would work at the church in the mornings and Tom in the afternoons. I would finish up my work by the end of the week. I went back to where I was staying and took a long hot shower.

The next morning I arrived at the church and there was a letter threatening me with a lawsuit. I gathered up my things and left. I told the secretary good-by. I went back to the house, packed my things, and told the woman I was staying with I was leaving and not to ask me why. I drove for fifteen hours, back to my extended family and rape-crisis counseling.

But it did not stop there. Tom continued to harass me with threatening letters and tried to make it so I would not be able to go to Zambia as a missionary.

There are those who say there is no such thing as date rape or spousal rape. Of course most of those who talk that way are men. Many men "just don't get it." They think, "She asked for it. She was wearing tight jeans and a see-through blouse." "If she didn't walk that way we wouldn't get so turned on." "She should know better than to be out on the streets at night, alone." These are just some of the remarks that are made about women who are raped. Rape is not about sex. It is about power and control. It is about using violence to gain power and control over women.

This same violence, for power and control, is found in the battering of wives and the abuse of children.

RICH OR POOR—VIOLENCE IS VIOLENCE

The income of a family does not determine if there is violence in the family, nor is the amount of education a determining factor. One night I called my friend Betty, only to be told by her daughter that her mother was in the hospital. I could hear yelling in the background as she hung up. There was only one hospital in town, so I got in the car and drove right over.

As I walked into Betty's room I could see the curtains were drawn around her bed. I peeked in and saw that she was awake and looking out the window. "Betty," I spoke gently, "I heard you were here and so I came to see you."

I didn't have to ask what had happened. Her face was one big bluish-purple mass. Her left arm was in a cast that was fastened to a body cast. Just as I started to speak again in rushed her husband Don. "What are you doing here?" he demanded. "Can't you see Betty needs her rest? She has been in a terrible accident." His voice was loud and shrill.

In walked the doctor. "Hello, Peggy!" he greeted me. "I am so glad you came to see Betty." We were all friends from the same couples group at the church. "Betty needs her friends to be with her." Taking Don by the arm the doctor led him out of the room. All I could hear was Don arguing that he was her husband and had a right to be there.

Even with reports from the doctor and statements from her daughters, Betty would not press charges. As she told me, "Who would believe that gentle looking, white-haired judge would ever beat his wife? No, I can't break up the home. The girls are still in grade school. How will it affect them?"

Betty went back home. I don't think she was ever beaten that severely again, but the abuse did continue. Don listened to the doctor and sought help, but the scars remained with Betty. The girls, too—now in high school—have been in therapy. They told me that their father had never hit them, but when he was angry at them he would hit their mother. When I asked them if they dated, they said no. I realized that the biggest scare for them is that they see all men as being like their father. After talking with our mutual doctor friend, we also talked with their pastor and worked on ways for the girls to have other male role models in their lives. One family invited the girls to spend time with them.

We talked with Betty about the effect Don's behavior was having on the girls. She realized that it would have been better to have left Don years ago because the girls now know only the bad part of their father. Betty is still protecting Don, but she is beginning to see the need to care about her daughters. When you are in the middle of an abusive situation, sometimes it is hard to call the shots right. You cannot see because you are so close to it.

A CALL IN THE NIGHT

I was reading in bed, as I usually do when home alone in the evenings. The phone rang and I thought, who could that be calling me at this hour. "Peggy," came a whispering quivering voice, "this is Evelyn. Joe is trying to break down the door to the house. Can you come over and help me?" I could hear little Natalie screaming and crying in the background.

"It will take me thirty minutes to get there. I am coming." Before I left, I called the police in her town and told them her husband was breaking his restraining order.

I lived in the middle of the San Fernando Valley in Los Angeles, and Evelyn lived in the northeast part of the Valley. We both worked for the same community service organization. She had come to work one day missing a tooth. I know now there had been days when she came with bruises, but with make-up she was able to cover them up.

When I got to her home, the police were there and Joe was in one of their cars. When he saw me get out of my car, he yelled at me out the car window, "You are the one who caused all the trouble! Why don't you white folks just leave us blacks alone?"

I walked up to the policeman at the door of the house and identified myself. When Evelyn heard my voice she came to the door. Little Natalie was clinging to her bathrobe. The medic had treated her cuts and was waiting for me, so I could take care of Natalie while she went to the hospital for tests to confirm spousal rape. Natalie and I followed along to the hospital and waited. Evelyn had asked if she and Natalie could come and stay with me that night.

Because we were both afraid that Joe would come to my place looking for her, I took her to some friends of mine for the night. She and Natalie lived with my two sons and me for two weeks while she was getting a complete security system installed. She filed charges of rape and assault that were upheld by the courts, and her divorce was granted while Joe was in prison.

Evelyn had lost one child through a miscarriage after one of Joe's beatings. That is when she kicked him out of the house and got a restraining order against him. He came back many times, but would always leave when he heard the police sirens. Evelyn had even asked the police to keep the lights and sirens off when they came to arrest him but they didn't. The only reason he had not left that night was because Evelyn told him that she had not called the police, and he did not know she had called me; they caught him literally with his pants down. He had blood on him as he came hobbling out of the house. Evelyn was behind him with a large cut on her arm. This time the police had to take her seriously. When they questioned what part I had to play in this situation, Evelyn spoke up: "She is the only one that believes me, that Joe has been beating me and threatening me and my child."

WHAT DOES IT ALL MEAN?

The need of husbands, boyfriends, men, to control women often takes on violent forms—rape and battering. We know that age, class, race, professional status, and economic income are not defining factors. We also know that even though many of these acts are cloaked in "love" or "sexual" language, rape and battering has nothing to do with either of these terms. As defined in chapter 12, rape and battering are both violent acts, acts of choice. Men are not out of their minds with jealousy; they are not acting out of uncontrollable rage; they are not temporarily insane. Men who rape and batter a woman know what they are doing, and it is premeditated. They are trying to control the woman. Don battered Betty because she was becoming more and more involved in local politics and he was not able to command every moment of her attention. Evelyn had begun working for the first time in her life as a trainee, and Joe suspected her of infidelity now that she was working with men. He felt threatened. Tom was not able to control me with sexual talk, so he tried to control me with sexual assault and rape. The compulsive need for power and control always leads to violence, whether it is in the family, community, nation, or world.

PART IV

RELIGIONS: OPPRESSIVE
OR LIBERATING?

17

Women's Deep Spirituality

As I listened to women telling their stories, I found in most of them a deep spirituality—a spirituality that was part of their whole being, not just something brought out when needed; it was not a crisis spirituality. Some of them knew the traditional ways of their religion were oppressive to women and therefore had moved away from those traditions, but not from their own spirituality—the center within themselves where they knew their God, regardless of what name they used. They found their spirituality deep within themselves and in the expression of other women.

Their spiritual stories were told through words, songs, prayers, movement, and gestures. What I learned most from them was the hope and vitality shared by these women. All religions have a basic core of beliefs. Many of them are the same beliefs, which have a moral and ethical premise. As religion is lived and practiced in a culture, it takes on many of the characteristics of that culture. Or could it be the other way around—the culture takes on the characteristics of the religion? Whichever way it is argued, usually the purity of the core becomes contaminated, with many different interpretations and expressions becoming part of the religion.

A good example of how religions are affected by cultural practices is provided by the Islamic religion. The Quran does not teach that women must be veiled, just that women must be modestly dressed, with only face and hands exposed. Some have taken the injunction further and required women to be completely veiled. In the Quran, women are equal to men, yet the stereotype of Muslim women is one of being oppressed and kept in the *purdah*,[1] which is true in some Islamic cultures. Yet in other parts of the Islamic culture women are encouraged to use their gifts and talents, to complete college and university training, to become professionals. Here in the United States, Muslim women have to overcome both the prejudice toward their faith plus the stereotypical concept that all Muslims are Arabs who follow all aspects of Arab culture.

As I indicated, changes and stereotypes develop when religion and culture meet and mix. The basic core teachings become blended with the culture, and the line between religion and culture becomes blurred. It is out of this blending and blurring that more and more prejudices and stereotypes develop. We all need to remember that moral and ethical principles, such as love, forgiveness, truth, honesty, dignity of persons, peace, and justice, are tenets of all great world religions.

As we listen to these women's stories, we should remember that they hold truth for them in the way their religious traditions and faiths have affected their lives. These stories may not reflect the basic core teachings of their religion, but they do reflect the way those teachings have been interpreted by them at this time and place in history.

The women in Africa suffer as they try to move from their traditional religion into a new religion, be it Islam or Christianity. They are caught between two worlds. A young woman who was the science teacher and a Christian at Njase, where I taught, was struggling with the death of her mother. As a friend and chaplain, I went to talk with her. She told me that her mother had died when lightning struck her hut. I had heard that a witch had cast a spell upon her. I asked if she believed this.

"I know I am not suppose to believe in witches, but why else would my mother's hut be hit by lightning and not the trees or other huts," she said.

As I asked more questions, I discovered that the hut sat on top of an anthill.[2] I also found out that her mother had run a coat hanger wire out of the pointed top of her hut to serve as an antenna for her radio, and that her mother had been sitting beside the radio. As I pointed these things out to her I asked, "As a scientist, what is the reason for your mother's death?"

She was able to see the logic behind the accident, but she still had trouble taking the step from witchcraft to scientific logic when it came to the death of her own mother.

Death carries with it very powerful magic—in some ways it is more powerful than birth. It is around these two major events that many religious traditions are found—traditions that women almost universally find oppressive for them. There are taboos related to normal body cycles of women and with the normal bodily processes of pregnancy and birth. These taboos usually lead to the oppression of females all of their lives. Because religious traditions and beliefs are so pervasive in a society and have such deep roots, any change takes time and much suffering on the part of those affected.

The stories from Africa all relate to religious belief in the evil death spirit. I am telling the stories of three different women who were affected by this belief to show this is not an isolated tradition, but one that affects women throughout the country of Zambia as well as in other African nations.

Women who are followers of Gandhi in India emphasize the positive relationship among them with a freshness that is expressed in their dancing and singing. Gandhian feminists exhibit the joy and hope that saturates their being; their very life. The *Harijans*, the untouchables, showed me an essence though they were poor economically, they were alive inside with the Truth: the Truth that they were valuable—that they mattered.

Historically the Hindu religion oppresses women. Over years and centuries its ethics—of nonviolence, love, and justice—have taken on a different texture. As often happens, the male has become the dominant theologian of the religion. The authority men have given themselves has become a power to oppress women and those who are different. The husband is worshiped as "the god," and wives show their deepest devotion to their husbands by committing *sati*, sacrificing themselves on their husband's burning fureral pyre. We also learned of the Hindu value of women in the stories of bride-burnings. Nowdays, Gandhian feminists are providing women of the Hindu faith a new way of looking at Hindu teachings.

Male domination and the patriarchal structure are seen in both the Catholic and the Protestant churches. Some may challenge this statement, yet they would be hard pressed to show where feminist structure—equal treatment—is written into church polity, let alone practiced. Even so at the grassroots there are changes being made.

The changes in the Catholic Church brought about by Vatican II in the 1960s led the Catholic churches in Latin America to hold two very important conferences—one in Medellin, Colombia, in 1968, and the other in Puebla, Mexico, in 1979. During this time both Catholic and Protestant theologians in Latin America began drawing attention to what was happening in Basic Christian Communities (BCC) throughout Latin America. The roles women were beginning to play in both the Catholic and the Protestant churches proved to be quite a radical change. Indeed the BCC itself was a radical change from anything that had gone before—so radical, in fact, many in the patriarchal structure were not willing to make the changes. As we have seen BCCs are a moving force in both rural and urban communities. It is often women, the ones carrying the double and triple burdens of oppression, who have found their greatest liberation through their own spirituality and have shared it with other women and with the community as a whole.

There are many different issues surrounding women and religion in the United States, but the one least often dealt with is the relationship of lesbians, their spirituality, and traditional religious institutions. I have known for several years the two women whose stories are shared here. Listening to their stories again caused me to reflect deeper into my own spirituality. Their faith in themselves and the love they have within themselves, a love they want to share, provides a time for rejoicing and for hope. But the institutional church continuously puts up roadblocks, roadblocks that hinder the ministry of lesbians and gay men, and this angers me.

18

Evil Death Spirit: Stories from Africa

Traditions[1] sometimes outlive the society in which they have existed as part of the culture. I saw this happening in Zambia. One tradition mandated that when a husband or father died the wife or mother was forced to leave her home and her children, taking with her only what she alone could wear and carry. Her brothers and sisters could not help her. At the school where I taught,[2] I saw this tradition from two different angles.

LET ME TAKE MY CHILDREN: ZAMBIA

The soft beating of the drums from the workers' compound became my lullaby soon after I arrived at the school. But the sound that woke me in the night was not the beating of drums, but an intermingling of moaning, wailing, and chanting. I got out of bed and wandered into the living room trying to figure out where the sound was coming from. Elizabeth, my housemate, was standing on the porch. "What is that sound?" I asked. "It seems to be coming from Deborah and Isaiah's house." Deborah was the school nurse and Isaiah was the accountant. Isaiah was also the one who helped the girls with their sports, netball games, and the track and field day.

"It is Isaiah," she said. "He died about a half an hour ago at the hospital from a blood clot on the brain." There was the steadiness in Elizabeth's voice that I had come to know, but on her cheek I could see a tear reflected in the light from the pole lamp.

"Dead! How could that be? I just talked with him this afternoon. We walked home together from the staff room." Disbelief surged through my body. I did not know it then, but death was to become a common visitor to our campus. That night was my first lesson on how old traditions and Christianity become assimilated into a new way of experiencing death.

"What is the sound? I asked again.

"That is wailing—the girls and faculty," she replied. I could see people sitting on the ground in the yard of Deborah's house. More and more girls came up the path from their dormitories. As each person arrived, the sound grew louder and louder. I realized that sleep for the night was over.

"Should we be over there also?" I asked, hoping the answer would be "no," yet wanting to be a part of it.

"No, that is their heathen way of responding to death. We as Christian missionaries cannot support their heathen ways." Elizabeth who had been a missionary in different parts of Africa all of her adult life, was to celebrate eighty years of life that day. Just then Joan, a young teacher from Iowa, came by to ask if I would like to go over to Deborah's with her. I did and I didn't want to. I looked at Elizabeth. She just turned and walked back into the house and into her room.

"I know Elizabeth thinks we should not take part in this, but I also know it will mean a lot to Deborah if we are there," Joan said.

My own curiosity got the better of me. "I will go over for a while. Let me get on a *chtangy*[3] and I will be with you."

As we walked across the road, I asked Joan, "What are we to do? Tell me and I will just follow you."

As we got to the edge of the yard, Sue, a young teacher from Canada, was waiting for us. "I don't think we can get into the house from the front, we will have to go around to the back," Sue said.

I could see what she meant. The yard was solid with girls. There was not even room to step between or over them. Each girl had a *chtangy* wrapped around her and a scarf on her head. They looked very different from the classroom, where their wore dark green uniforms, white socks and black shoes.

As we walked to the back yard we were faced with the same problem, a sea of bobbing heads with waves of wailing washing over us. "We will just have to try to get through," Joan said.

We inched our way to the corner of the house and then clung to the side as we stepped over, around, and sometimes on the girls. As we reached the back door, we were greeted with a sound that almost washed us back into the yard. The house was as full as the yard.

"We will never get into to see Deborah," Sue said. "Maybe we should just wait until morning and come over then. I think I will go back to the house and cook up the chicken I got yesterday in Choma so I can bring it over when it is daylight. Maybe by then the girls will have gone back to the dining room to eat." We all left.

The next morning Sue stopped by so we could go over to the house together. I had baked some of the brownies I knew Deborah liked so much. The wailing had continued and I had become accustomed to it. As we stepped out the front door, I could not believe what I saw. "How are we ever going to get over there?"

I asked. "People are even out here in the road."

"We are not going over to Deborah's house. She is over at Endless's now," Sue replied.

As we walked by Deborah's house, I could see men inside taking things down from the walls. All of the furniture seemed to be on the front porch. The house looked bare through the windows. There were no curtains, no lamp in the window, and even the flowers outside the door had been cut down.

"Why is she at Endless's? Why is all the furniture on the porch? What is going on inside of the house?" My childhood "Why's?" were flooding out of my brain and my mouth was having trouble keeping up.

"I have not been here long enough to know all the answers but I am sure that Endless, or Paul and Martha, can answer your questions," Sue said.

As we came closer to Endless's house, we could hear wailing there also. A subterranean rumbling roar seemed to rise up from the very center of the earth and permeate the whole of life. We could feel the sound waves against our bodies. When the girls saw us coming they scooted together to make a narrow path for us to walk up to the door. Inside, Deborah sat on the couch. Alone. There was a stillness here that I had not heard since I had been awakened in the night. The door and all the windows were shut. I walked over and sat down beside her. I did not know the customs but I knew Deborah needed love. I put my arm around her shoulder and took her hand in mine. Her red eyes looked up at me and there was a great sigh as she grabbed hold of me and began wailing. Endless came into the room from the kitchen where Sue had taken the food. Endless's eyes were wide with shock, I think, or maybe it was anger. They turned just as quickly to compassion. Out of my own compassion and innocence I had broken a taboo.

I learned that the wife of the deceased was cast out of her house upon the death of her husband with only what she could wear and carry. A friend or family member could allow her to come into their house, but they were not to touch her. She has an evil spirit in her and until she has it cast out she is not to be touched—and there I sat holding Deborah. Both Endless and Deborah were Christians, as was Isaiah and his family, but old ways die hard.

I asked, "Where is little Isaiah and Loveness?" Deborah's wailing erupted with such force that I was thrown against the back of the couch. Sue was shaking her head and her hand in a "no-no" sign. Endless came and sat beside us. She told Deborah that we had brought some food and asked her to please drink some tea and eat one of the brownies I had made. Sue and I stayed until we were able to get Deborah to lie down for awhile. Endless went outside and told the girls to remain, if they liked, but to quiet the wailing because Deborah was resting now.

Sue stopped by my home with me. Elizabeth had prepared tea and some sweets for us.[4] Paul and Martha, our next-door neighbors, were there. I asked them my "Why" questions and they explained the tradition regarding the wife/mother.

"The house is cleared out of everything to let the evil spirit of death go out. They do not want anything there it can hide in. The wife/mother is sent away with only what she can carry because everything belongs to her husband's family. Besides, she could have the evil death spirit in her. She might have wanted her husband dead. Because everything belongs to the husband, the children stay with his family. Even when the mother is working and could support them," Paul explained.

Martha then told how women were trying to change this custom. "We want to keep our good traditions, like the importance of the family and virginity, but this one we are trying to change. We can now have wills, but if the husband's family gets to the home first after a death, they will take all the valuables away before the wife's family can help her protect her rights."

"Doesn't Deborah have a brother living in Choma? Didn't he get here to help her?" I asked.

"Yes, she has a brother in Choma, but he was up in Lusaka yesterday. Anyway Isaiah's brother arrived last night for a visit. In fact it was only about an hour after I saw his lorry[5] drive up that Deborah came running over with the children saying Isaiah was sick and they were taking him to the hospital," Paul said. "I went over and went with them. Isaiah died soon after we got there. They said it was a blood clot in the brain. I couldn't believe it, but the brother-in-law was not going to let Deborah ride back home in his lorry. I had to remind him that Deborah did not have the evil death spirit in her. I had to remind him he was a Christian and shouldn't believe in the evil death spirit any more. He finally agreed to let her ride in the back of the lorry. He told her she could go into the house and get whatever she could wear and carry and then she had to leave the house. She came over to our house where the children were. I sent Martha over to get Endless. Endless came and got Deborah. She has been with Endless ever since she took her home."

"Didn't Isaiah have a will?" Sue asked. "I remember him telling Joan and me he was going to make sure Deborah got the car and the furniture because she had worked just as hard as he had for the family."

"Deborah told her brother-in-law that Isaiah had a will, but the brother-in-law would not listen to her. He has already sent the children away. When he came over to our home to get them, I was not going to let him in because Deborah was still there. He knocked me down, stormed into the living room, and grabbed Loveness off the pad where she was sleeping and tore little Isaiah out of Deborah's arms. I picked up a stick of wood to hit him, but he was holding the children in such a way that I could not hit him any place but on the legs without hitting the children. He stormed out of the house, put the children in the lorry with the things he had loaded up, and drove off. Deborah did say she had gotten the copy of the will out of the house. I have the copy Isaiah gave to me to keep. I am going to go into Choma today to see what we can do about it. The problem is that most police will not do anything about family matters like this."

Deborah remained at the school for the rest of the term. Her children had not been returned to her when she moved closer to her own family. She was not able to get the money out of their joint bank account because of her brother-in-law.

She had no money to pay a lawyer, so she was unable to go to court. She was given the money from Isaiah's pension fund that the church had set up for the school staff, but that was not very much. She was able to work, but her grief and pain made it hard for her to hold a job. Losing her husband and her children was almost more than she could bear.

Endless knew her pain. She, too, had lost her children at the time of her husband's death. It took Endless five years before she was able to get her children back. All of this time Endless taught at the school and was capable of caring for her children, but was prevented by tradition from having them with her. Her mother-in-law was able to get the children returned to Endless.

I MUST SPEAK OUT: ZAMBIA

Grace was the "head girl" of the students at Njase. She had entered every speech contest since coming to Njase four-and-a-half years before and had won first place every time. She had three times advanced to the top five in the country and won first at the nationals the last two years. Elizabeth had been her coach each year.

Elizabeth very seldom raised her gentle voice, but when she did, her British accent became so thick that it was hard not to hear her if you were within a hundred feet of her. I was walking down the porch of the classroom building where Elizabeth's office was, when I heard this unmistakable voice. "No Grace, you cannot talk on that subject; the judges are all men. This is too controversial a subject for the contest," Elizabeth was exclaiming.

"I don't care! The men in this country need to be educated on this subject," Grace was saying.

"Ha! You two, slow down a bit. Miss Howard, you are going to raise your blood pressure. Just what is all this about?" I asked.

"Grace wants to use the question of widows losing their children for her speech contest," Elizabeth said.

"Do you have to use the same subject at each level of the contest, or can each speech be on a different subject?" I asked.

"Well, I guess they can be on different subjects, but the girls usually give the same speech at each level," Elizabeth responded.

"Check out the rules and if she can have different subjects then pick a neutral topic for each of the lower levels and save the bombshell for the finals," I suggested.

"But what if I don't win at each level? You know sometimes when a girl has won so many times before, they give the honor to some other person," Grace explained.

"Well, you will be so good that there is no way they could give the honor to anyone else," I said. "I understand you are the tops."

"It is because Miss Howard is such a good coach, that is the reason I win," Grace said.

"Now, Miss Howard, that is high praise for you. Aren't you ashamed of yourself for yelling at Grace?" I teased.

"I was not yelling. Ladies don't yell. I may have raised my voice to make a point but I don't yell," Elizabeth answered with all the dignity of an English lady.

Grace was able to speak on two different topics, so she saved her speech on "The Rights of Widows to Their Children" until the national finals. There was no question, Grace was the best, but Elizabeth had been right. All the judges were men and they marked Grace down on subject matter, so she came in last. The media was not as conservative. They asked Grace for a copy of her speech and ran it in the daily newspaper. The school received praise from women and the more progressive men and "flak" from traditional conservative men. Grace went on to the university and continued her feminist activities.

Traditions often have to do with powers greater than ourselves. Religious traditions come out of the needs of the society. The tradition of the widow losing her home and her children because she has an evil spirit that caused her husbands death came out of the need to explain why the head of the household, the husband, would die before the wife, the servant of the household.

Later I was visiting with Grace's Aunt Ruth in Livingstone after I moved there to teach at David Livingstone College. She knew of Grace's speech, which I had read, but there were still some questions about the need for this tradition that were unanswered for me. Aunt Ruth's father had been a medicine man before he was converted to Christianity, and he had told Ruth many of the stories of their tribal traditions. One of these stories Aunt Ruth passed on to me.

EVIL BLOOD SPIRIT: ZAMBIA

"Men did not understand how women functioned. They thought, because we flow blood every month, evil was in us. They thought when the flow of blood stopped when we were pregnant, we had gotten rid of the evil. Many of us do not begin to have a flow of blood again until after we stopped nursing the baby. As long as we do not have the flow of blood we have no evil in us. We are very highly revered," she began.

"What about older women who have gone through menopause and have stopped flowing blood because of their age, are these women also thought to be evil or are they revered?" I asked.

"As you know most of us do not live many years after the flow of blood stops, some not even that long. Most of the children are grown, so the tradition of taking everything and the children does not happen. If the husband dies young and tradition is followed the wife will move back with her own family or tries to make it on her own. If the husband dies after the flow of blood stops she usually moves in with a son or daughter."

It was still not clear to me why the flow of blood was evil. "Are all kinds of blood evil? What about blood of animals when they are killed? What about blood when a person is hurt? Are these also evil?"

"Yes and no. The blood from a cut is letting evil out of the person. That person has to let the blood flow freely to get all the evil out. A nurse friend of mine has told me she sometimes has trouble stopping the bleeding because the hurt person, or his or her family, wants them to bleed to let the evil all out. If the person, bleeds to death they say the person had too much evil inside.

"Now blood from animals that are killed, no, that is not evil blood because they have killed the animal for food. But if a wounded animal gets blood on a person then that person has to go through a cleansing ritual.

"Blood is a very powerful thing in our old traditions. Those of us who have become Christians find it is sometimes hard to put aside our old way of thinking. But many of the women, like my niece Grace, see what the old ways are doing to us and that we must free ourselves from them. It is not we women who have the evil in us, it is the old ways of thinking and treating women that is evil. Schools like Njase and colleges like the one here in Livingstone help us to learn to trust ourselves. We learn to trust that we are God's children and true daughters equal with our brothers."

Still I questioned, "So the men think when a husband dies it is because the wife, who has evil death spirit in her, has killed him. Are you saying that they think that when a woman is pregnant and giving birth—giving life—she does not have evil death in her then? What about the blood at the time of birth?" I asked.

"That is evil coming out with life," Aunt Ruth explained. "That is why the baby has to be washed the first thing. When the woman passes the afterbirth she has gotten all of the evil out of her.

"You know it is men who have thought up all of these traditions and we women have accepted them, but we are learning more about our bodies. We know the flow of blood is a natural function of our womanhood. That is why we are putting aside the traditions that are against women. And most of the traditions are against women. Some of the missionary men tried to tell us we were not as good as men, but as we learned to read, we read the first chapter in Genesis before the second chapter. So we learned we were equal before we learned we were created to serve Adam and caused evil. We read about Jesus and how he treated women as equals before we read about Paul and how women are to be submissive, so we learned what it means to be equal with men. We are learning we are not evil and we are not our husbands' servants, but God's servants and there is a big difference.

"Our traditional ways are changing because we women are changing. Our new religion supports us if we don't let the men tell us what Christianity is to mean. We are learning for ourselves. We are becoming our true selves."

Aunt Ruth and I had many visits the year I was teaching at the college. I learned many things about traditional religion and how her faith and her life were one.

19

Expressing Their Spirituality:
Stories from Asia

GANDHIAN HINDUISM IS FEMINIST: INDIA

Madras, India, can be an awesome city when the visitor is there for the first time and all alone. Someone met me in Bombay and took me where I wanted to go, but in Madras I was on my own. I went to the Hotel Victoria and checked into my room. It was only ten in the morning and my bus did not leave until the next afternoon. When I asked for directions, the hotel clerk looked at me with questioning eyes, and tried to direct me to the temples and uptown shopping area. When I insisted on going to the marketplace, he gave in and gave me a crude map that at least pointed me in the right direction. As always, my hotel was close to the train station so if I got lost I could make signs and gestures telling people I needed to get to the station and then I could find my way back. I also picked up a hotel card just in case. I stepped out into the steamy heat of an April morning not sure what I would find, but looking for the market and women.

I was beginning to become accustomed to the masses of people in India. African city streets are not as crowded, and the poor are usually found in squatter camps, not living on the streets as in Bombay and Madras. As I began to walk, I soon came to a small park. I could hear singing, so I moved toward the crowd that had gathered. When the singing stopped, a woman in a silk *sari* with gold earrings and a briefcase began to speak. She had flashing black eyes and a long thick braid down her back with jasmine flowers tucked in at the base of her head. I moved closer to the small platform on which she was standing. When she finished, there was more singing and she stepped down right in front of me. "You are a visitor to our city, but you are not like most visitors. You have come to where the poor people are and not to our famous temples and tourist bazaars. Why is this?" she asked.

Her English and her accent took me back to Njase Girls School in Zambia and to Lila Johnson, one of our Indian teachers. "I am on my way home to the United States from teaching for three years in Zambia, as a missionary. I am spending some time in India on the way. I am very interested in women and want to listen and learn what I can in the twenty-some hours I will be in Madras before I take a bus to my next destination. My name is Peggy," I said as I extended my hand for a handshake.

As she took my hand I could feel her warmth welcoming me. "You can call me Kan. My full name is too hard for even my friends to pronounce. I don't have to be to the office until two this afternoon. Why don't you come with me and I will introduce you to some women? This evening you are invited to my home where you can talk with more women if you like."

With that we headed down a small alley-like street. The cobblestones were slick with the waste water that had been thrown out the doors and windows. We turned a sharp corner and went through an archway. There before me was a garden that defied the filth we had just come through. In one corner of the garden was a bench.

"You wait there," Kan said as she pointed to the bench, "and I will go and find Mohsina. She can help you talk with the women who will be arriving here soon."

I sat in the shade of a tree, in deep thought, listening to a bird singing as the fragrance of jasmine bathed my being. What peace there was in this place. A true sanctuary from what was just around the corner, in the outside life.

"You like our small peace?" The voice was as gentle as the garden where I sat. At first I thought she meant "piece of land," but as Mohsina told me about the garden I knew she meant the "peace" that we all search for within ourselves.

"I felt the sacredness of this place as we walked in. What peace! What fullness! I am not sure just how to express what I feel."

Mohsina smiled, her white teeth lighting up her walnut-brown face. "We call this place *Shanti*—which is the Sanskrit word for your word peace. But we do not mean simply no fighting, we mean the inner peace found within ourselves," she explained. "Kan told me you wanted to learn from and listen to women. Soon the women from the market will be coming here during the heat of the day when the markets close down. We will have a *bhajan mandalis*, 'circle of song singing,' some songs tell stories and others are hymns or religious songs. I will try to explain what the stories mean. I am sure the women will want to know about you. What can I tell them?" she asked.

I thought, what do I say to these women? I don't want them to focus on me. I want them to do what they always do when they come here. "Just tell them I am happy to be with them today. I am here to be a part of their time and life and to learn from them. I am not a newspaper reporter nor a writer, I am just a woman wanting to learn from other women," I told Mohsina.[1]

The women came in chanting, clapping, and dancing. It was a clapping rhythm I was never able to do. It is so different from either the African or the American rhythms. I knew it was not a planned performance but a spontaneous expression reflecting a part of their lives. I had told Mohsina not to introduce me, but to tell them about me only if they asked.

In front of the bench where we were sitting was an open area of smooth cobblestones. The women gathered there. The chanting and movement reminded me of the grace of the Russian Bolshoi Ballet. "They are chanting a song of joy for life," Mohsina said.

As the women finished their movement each gracefully sat, forming a circle. Mohsina motioned for me to join her and the women in the circle. There was chattering and laughter as each woman brought some food out of the folds of her *sari* and placed it on a banana palm leaf that had been placed in the middle. Mohsina brought two small round breads and two oranges out of the small cloth bag she had placed beside her. I looked at her with embarrassment since I had nothing to offer. She smiled and handed me a loaf and an orange that I placed in the middle.

Before the women began to eat, there was more singing. "They are singing a song of thanksgiving now. They know that each has very little, but together they have enough," Mohsina said.

There was so little food I did not want to take any, yet I knew if I did not join in, I would offend them. I picked up a small thin cake with a shiny glaze. It was delicious. One of the younger women offered me a large banana. I was not sure what to do. It was the largest piece of food there. I knew that this might be the only meal the women would have. Just then Mohsina handed me a small knife. I took it and cut the banana into four pieces, keeping only one for myself. There was much chattering and laughter, and I asked Mohsina if I had done something wrong.

"No! They are saying you eat very little for such a big woman." It was then I realized that most of the women there were about five feet tall and weighed maybe a hundred pounds. I laughed and said, "I am the size I am because I eat too much. I need to learn to eat less."

During the meal the women asked who I was. Mohsina told them, and immediately the young woman who had given me the banana stood up in the middle of the circle and began to sing, clap, and dance to me.

"What did you tell them? Why she is dancing for me?" I asked.

"She is singing, 'A friend has come a long way to visit us and we are honored to have such a visitor.'"

"Is there a way I can tell them I am the honored one?" I asked.

"Do you have a dance or song you could do?" Mohsina asked.

"No, I am afraid we do not have such beautiful customs in my country. But I do love to dance. Maybe I could create one for them." I slipped out of my sandals and pulled my *chtangy* out of my large purse and got up as gracefully as I could. I had done interpretative dance while I was in Zambia. My students loved to express themselves through dance. As I began to move I felt clumsy, but as I meditated on what I wanted to tell them, my body became more relaxed and fluid. As I moved, weaving the cloth among the women, I soon felt like we were one.

After more singing and dancing, the women returned to their market stalls. Mohsina and I followed them out into the afternoon heat. The garden was so refreshing I had forgotten how stale and stifling the heat can be in an open market. As Mohsina and I walked and talked I knew I had learned more from the women that afternoon than I ever could have from reading a book. Their songs told of how important it was to be self-reliant, yet to work together. How peace was found within oneself and not outside. How it took more courage to stand for what was just and right than to act in violence.

We returned to the garden, later when Kan came to take me to her home for dinner I asked her how Gandhi and his teachings had affected women in India. She told me there was a group of women coming over in the evening to meet me and they could tell me many things about Gandhi. They were all his followers. Kan herslef was a widow who now ran her late husband's business. Before his death she was very active as a Gandhian feminist, working with poor women like the ones in the market. She and her friends had provided the *Shanti* garden where I had been in the afternoon. As a business woman Kan had not become part of a retreat *ashram*,[2] although she met with women to carry on their work with women, especially poor women.

The ten women who joined us on the veranda for supper were part of a women's group, Gandhian feminists. They were devout Hindus who followed the teachings of Mahatma Gandhi regarding the treatment of women, which are very different from the traditional Hindu treatment. Some say Gandhi was a reformer as much as he was a revolutionary. The women of India have found in his teachings a way to liberate themselves and still remain in family and community.

That evening the women put structure and words to what I had experienced in the afternoon with the women in the garden. We are all aware of Gandhi's belief in nonviolence. The two—Gandhi and nonviolence—are often considered synonymous. But that was not the only interpretation of Hindu teaching Gandhi lifted up. Individual autonomy—self-realization—was stressed through self-reliance and self-control. This positive sense of one's own self was one of the key elements for the Gandhian feminists. These women made sure I understood that this focus on the self was not isolated individualism. They insisted it is only through knowing oneself that one is able to relate in a healthy way to the family and to society.

The Hindu Code Bill, which would have allowed all religions to be governed in the civil courts with the same laws, was one of the bills the women worked hardest for in Pre-Independent India. They felt it was important that Hindus, Muslims, and Christians be treated equally. It was the religious conservative men who carried the most influence, then and still today. The bill was not passed.

"I think you experienced *bhajan mandalis,* this afternoon," Kan said. She told the women she had taken me to the *Shanti* garden. "Singing prayers is a part of each of our gatherings," explained Kan. "This evening, when it is cooler, we will go into the garden and spend time in singing prayers. Gandhi had many different kinds of prayer songs he taught us. One day I was with a Christian friend in her home. I heard her daughter singing a song. It was one that we often sing; I learned it was from your Bible. Gandhi, you know, was involved with Christianity when he lived in South Africa. We also use Muslim and Sikh prayers. If the prayers are about universality of religion, equality, and solidarity, we use them. One song we sing is from your civil-rights movement, *We Shall Overcome*. Even though we have our independence from Great Britain, we women are not free yet. This is the way it often happens; once the political liberation comes, women's issues and rights are forgotten. This is why so many Hindu women are what we call Gandhi feminists, because we know his teachings, of self-reliance and self-control, community and cooperation, have not been totally assimilated into our society."

By this time the western sky was orange with ink-etched trees silhouetted along the horizon. One woman began to sing and others joined in as we moved off the veranda and out into the coolness of the garden. The breeze bathed us in the essence of jasmine as nightingales began to woo us. The women's voices became part of a sinfonia as the evening opened into an opera of movement and music. The flow of bodies and *saris* metamorphased from a three-dimensional sea of color, accented with the golden rays of the sunset, to flat black figures, seeking in the darkness for a new and different light. Just as the last rays bid adieu in the west, a new and silvery light began to return color to the figures. There was a resurrection of life as the moon rose higher and higher. We all became a part of the opera of life.

The next morning Kan picked me up at the hotel just as the sun was taking the place where the moon had been the night before. As we drove out of Madras and into the countryside, the pageant of life had begun. As we drew near the small earthen huts, a mass of humanity flooded from every doorway and raced down to the road. The sound of our car broke the stillness of the morning. As we left the car and moved toward the small street that ran down the middle of the cluster of huts, it was as if we were being carried on a brown wave surging with such force we could do nothing but be swept along with it. White teeth provided the only color in the surf of brown nakedness. As we approached the largest hut, two rooms instead of one, the wave of children turned us toward the door. Standing there in a white *sari*, face etched with lines, eyes deep set, and hands permanently crooked, was a woman whose smile was as warm as the sun. As she bowed and invited us in Kan whispered to me, "She is the teacher of the *ashram*. Her name is Sushil."

Kan had told me only that she was taking me to a village where I would meet some very interesting women. As we entered the room, I could hear a humming sound, but my eyes could not see in the dimly lit room. The door we had come through and the one leading to the back garden were the only sources of light. As we passed through the room, I saw a spinning wheel near the door. In the garden the women were busy with the morning work. Sushil led us to a group of benches under a tree where we sat and talked. I could see all of the garden from there and watched the activities of the morning. I am sure there were times when I missed what was being said because I was fascinated with the women working there. They all had on soft white *saris*. The cloth was not of fine texture but had the warmth and softness of homespun, which it was.

Sushil drew my attention back to the conversation as she began to speak in the elegance of the Queen's English that I had come to love hearing from Elizabeth, my fellow teacher in Zambia. Sushil had studied in England and as a young student had worked at one time for the British government.

"Kan tells me you have a keen interest in women and especially Gandhian feminists," Sushil said.

"Yes, I have. I did not know the term, Gandhian feminist, until yesterday, but Kan and her wonderful women friends have taught me many things. I am just sorry I have such a short time here," I replied.

"Well, we must make the most of it," she continued. "Let me say first it is an honor to have you with us today. We will share our lives with you. We are seekers of knowledge and Truth. For Gandhi, Truth was God. He sought that Truth through nonviolence. At one time he would have said God was Truth, but he came to realize Truth is God."

As the three of us sat on the benches under the tree, I felt I was in the presence of Sophia, the embodiment of wisdom. Sushil told me that some Hindus question the issue of separatism as a means to obtaining equality. She referred to our black power—civil rights—movement and those who felt that separatism was an obstacle to equality. She also talked about embracing the *Harijans*. She said Gandhi called them "children of God."

"We believe that all colors, castes, and creeds are equal within the Truth," she stressed. "The discrimination against untouchables is something that we have abhorred from the beginning. Many women were also treated in this way, as *goth*, as cows. We in the *ashrams* and all who follow Gandhi's teachings will always be working nonviolently for the equal acceptance of all people."

Kan reminded me that if I was going to catch my bus we would have to leave. Sushil motioned for one of the women who had come to join us to go into the hut. We met her as we reached the door. With a deep bow she handed me a tray covered with a white cloth. Beneath the cloth were several brass bowls of food.

"Please take this with you for your meal. And, Peggy, please keep the bowls as our gift to you," Sushil said.

The trip back seemed all too fast. As Kan helped me with my backpack, she gave me a hug. "I don't often do that. It is not part of our tradition but I know you American women often hug each other, and I wanted you to know what a blessing you have been to me."

The tears in my eyes reflected what was in my heart. Words were not needed to communicate. Hugs and tears said it all.

The early afternoon sun filtered through the dust in the air as I climbed aboard the bus and found a seat. Kan stood waving as we pulled out. I leaned my head back and closed my eyes, savoring the memory of the last twenty-eight hours as I ran my finger around the edge of the small brass bowl and ate the last of the curry rice.

20

Spirituality Is Their Liberation:
Stories from Latin America

We have already been introduced to Basic Christian Communities (BCC) and how these groups have helped women to find ways to address their problems. Now we are going to look more closely at BCC and see the role that women play within them and how they provide opportunities for women to experience God and express their faith in more feminine ways.

WIDOWS—YOUNG AND OLD ALIKE: GUATEMALA

We were later than we had planned. It was twilight by the time we arrived in the small village just west of Guatemala City where we were to have supper. The civil patrol had stopped us twice as we traveled back toward Guatemala City from Quezaltenango. Travelers on the highways were often questioned by the civil patrol if their presence seemed unusual. Two VW vans full of Anglos certainly counted as unusual travelers. Julio, our Quiche guide, was accustomed to this; as a Native Indian, he was always questioned when he traveled.

As we gathered in the small church hall I said to my friend Betty, "Where are the menfolk?" There were only elderly men there, whose craggy faces looked as if they could tell stories of generations of suffering and struggle. Each sat with his hands resting on a cane held between his legs. Loose cotton pants hung limply over their bony knees giving what little shape there was to the pants. Children were everywhere. Some of the babies played on a cloth close to the elderly men, whose eyes would dart a glance to check on them and then look straight ahead. Each seemed to have his own cluster of children to look after. If need be, a word would bring a child back on the cloth. Small boys had been playing in the churchyard as we drove up, and girls were helping their mothers with the food. But where were the older boys, the fathers, the husbands?

Julio was talking with one of the women when I went up to him. When he turned to me, I asked, "Julio, I don't see any fathers or husbands. There are no teenage boys. Where are all the men?"

"This BCC is made up of widows and a few elderly couples," he replied. "This whole community is mostly widows. Their husbands have either been killed, disappeared, fled to your country or Mexico, are hiding here in Guatemala, or have been taken by the civil patrol. This is one of the reasons I have brought you here, so you can see how the women have lived through the years of civil strife."

That evening we enjoyed the fellowship of these women and listened to their stories.

"We know God loves us and takes care of us even though we have lost our husbands and our children have no fathers," Juanita began. "We know because it is not God who has done this to us, it is the government. We know we will survive because we know love is more powerful than violence."

"One day the civil patrol came to our village in the mountains. They had guns and we were afraid, but we also knew there was nothing we could do to stop them," Rosa explained. "Then my grandmother walked out to where they were with a bucket of water and a gourd dipper and offered the boys some water. These were boys from a neighboring village. After she gave them some water—their guns pointed at her all the time—she offered them something to eat. We didn't have much, and we knew they would take it. But my grandmother offered it before they could ask for it. I am not sure if it was her lack of fear of them, her offering of water and food, or what, but they did not take the food, instead they turned and left. As they left they raised their guns and shot in the air toward the mountain. At first we thought they had seen some of the boys who had fled to the mountain when word came that the civil patrol was on its way. But the last boy in the line smiled a thank you and said, 'Our leaders had to hear some shots.'"

Carla could not have been much over eighteen or nineteen. She picked up her baby from one of the cloths on the floor and spoke as she was nursing it. "My husband, Manuel, fled the country after his two brothers, who were teaching people to read, had been killed. Manuel was a delegate of the word[1] in our village and had missed being killed because he was visiting a family who lived further up on the mountain. The civil patrol leader told Manuel's father he was lucky that day that they only killed two of his sons. They would get the other one next time.

"After the civil patrol left, I sent my sister up the trail to gather firewood and to leave the signal for Manuel not to come into the village until after dark. By the time he came home, I had prepared him some food and his change of clothing. I told him what had happened and he must leave that very night. Manuel's father came over with some money he had gathered from the villagers. His father told Manuel where he could find an uncle in Quezaltenango who could help him get over into Chiapas, Mexico, and on up to your country. Manuel has never seen his child."

Lew, one of the men in my group, asked, "How do you keep your faith? I am not sure I could. As a pastor I am to lead, but I wonder if I would have the faith to lead if I were here."

An elderly woman had sat down by her husband. As she spoke, we could see the love in the couple's eyes as they looked at each other. She answered Lew, "Faith is not something for me to keep. It is a gift from God. Jesus showed us how to love. As we love each other, including our enemy, the civil patrol, we know there is only one place the love can come from—God. When we share that love, we also have the gift of believing in where this love comes from."

I'm like Lew, I am not sure whether my love is full enough to have the gift of faith, but there was no question in any of our minds that night these women shared their love with us. Like all things of the spirit, one cannot really define it or even know it. It just is.

SEVEN YEARS OF FREEDOM: NICARAGUA

We were in Esteli to take part in the seventh anniversary of the freedom of Nicaragua. We had traveled all night. The day was hot but our spirits were high. This was the first year for the celebration to be held outside of Managua, the capitol. During this celebration I began to understand the zeal of the Nicaraguan people for their freedom and what liberation means to them. We had visited our own embassies in Guatemala City and Managua. We had talked with government officials in both countries and would do the same in El Salvador when we visited there. But now we were seeing and hearing the people celebrate what they deeply felt and believed.

The following Sunday we took part in three different religious responses to the freedom/liberation of Nicaragua. In the early morning we attended a mass, said by Archbishop Obando y Bravo in a church located in the affluent section of Managua. That church was being used in place of the cathedral that was damaged in the 1972 earthquake and had never been repaired. This service was attended by the wealthy and by middle-class business-people who had remained in Nicaragua after the fall of Somoza. The archbishop's sermon was about how God helps those who help themselves and blesses them.

In the afternoon we met with Rev. Norman Bent of the Moravian Church. This church is the strongest on the east coast among the Miskito Indians, and they also have a congregation in Managua. Most of the members of the congregation live near the church. They gathered for a special afternoon with us. They told of how they had been persecuted by Somoza and how they were now working with the government to improve their conditions. The Latin culture was different from their Indian culture, and they agreed that both cultures had a lot to learn from each other. Betty asked one of the women, "Are women treated differently now than they were treated before the liberation of Nicaragua?"

"Now we are able to be a part of the community," she answered. "We have a say in what is happening. Our Bible studies show us that liberation is for all people from all forms of oppression—oppression from the government, oppression from tribal leaders, oppression from men, oppression from our husbands. We knew this before, but we could not act out our faith in Jesus as the liberator because we were under a very heavy oppressor. The Somoza oppression filled every part of our lives. We are still working for our liberation. Sometimes the government is still oppressive, but now it is because they do not understand. They want to understand, where Somoza did not care."

Diana, a young college student in our group, questioned if Liberation Theology had changed their way of believing. A young woman student responded to her question: "When I read Gutierrez's *A Theology of Liberation* I realized he was putting into words what we had been thinking about and doing. You might say we had been practicing Liberation Theology, but had not put a name to it. We see in the Bible the message of liberation. We see it in the Old Testament in the Exodus story and in the prophets. We hear Jesus proclaiming it when he tells why he came and Mary proclaiming it when she sang about the coming of her baby. We, as women, see that we can be liberated, as we study the relationships Jesus had with women.

"There are people in your government in the United States who think our seeking liberation is communism. I am not sure just what communism is. I do know that as we study the Bible and we work with the people for better education and health care, so farmers can have their own land, and so workers can make a living wage, we see how we are doing what the Bible teaches us to do. We don't want to have to fight. We don't want this war that your country is supporting. We want to live our own lives, our own way, and have peace. That is what our faith teaches us and that is what we want for our country. Please tell your government to let us also be free and independent. Just as you fought for your independence and then had to build your nation, so we fought for ours. Now we need to build our nation."

That evening we attended the barrio church, Nuestra Senora de Los Angeles. Here was a congregation alive with music, singing, and a mass that involved the people. We were surrounded by beautiful murals depicting their lives, their struggles, their victories. As we saw in Guatemala, it was women, small children, and old men who were left to gather in a public place. Here, young girls, boys, and men were again fighting for their freedom. That night as the mothers, each in turn, called out the names of their lost sons, or daughters, or husbands to be remembered, the unity of the congregation in their response of *Presente* told me that the unity was not just in their voices but also in their faith.

The somber formality of Archbishop Obando y Bravo's service; the involvement of the Moravians in their liberation of life, solidly based in their faith; and the unity in the voices and suffering expressed by the women at the mass gave me much to ponder in my own heart.

THERE IS A DIFFERENCE IN HOW YOU STUDY: COSTA RICA

When my group finished our study tour in El Salvador, I flew on to Costa Rica to continue my studies for two weeks at the Seminario Biblico Latinoamericano, in San José. Guillermo Cook was my host. Next door to the seminary were the offices of Latin American Evangelical Center for Pastoral Studies (CELEP) where Guillermo had his office. Even though it was summer, classes were being held at the seminary. However, most of my learning took place around the dining table, in the student lounge, and on trips with Guillermo. It was here, also, that I was able to become acquainted with Elsa Tamez, biblical studies professor at the seminary.

One of the starkest contrasts I experienced in the understanding and expression of Christianity came on my visit to Costa Rica. There, I found the more conservative theological expression of the Bible as well as those who expressed their biblical faith through Liberation Theology. The first Sunday I was there, I walked to the large Protestant church I had seen as I came into the city the evening before. The architecture, the interior design, the art, the music, the prayers, and the sermon were all very North American—conservative North American. The missionaries had done their job well in transplanting Protestant religion to Latin America.

That evening Guillermo took me to a BCC service. What a contrast! The service was held in a new housing development. The residents were building their own cinderblock houses and helping each other, a real communal effort. Each house had two or three rooms. Most of the cooking was done out of doors, and the houses were used for sleeping and sometimes eating if it rained.

Costa Rica was not in any kind of civil strife like her neighbors to the north, so there were both women and men at the service. I was introduced as a guest and was enjoying the singing, the music, and the warmth of being there—so different from the austere morning service. As Guillermo stood up, he took hold of my arm and spoke softly, "They want to hear from you. I told them you were a seminary student. They expect you to preach them a sermon."

This was one time when my experiences in Zambia came in handy, since this sort of thing happened often to me over there. Plus I was used to preaching with an interpreter. I told Guillermo he would have to interpret for me since I could not preach in Spanish. Aware that preaching in BCC was more like a Bible discussion or dialogue, I asked if there was a scripture passage that they were using that evening. He told me no, I could pick my own. By this time we were in front of the gathering of people. One of my favorite passages came to mind, John 4:1-32, the Samaritan Woman at the Well. I also thought there was more than enough in that passage to carry me through the evening. Guillermo told me I had an hour but could take more if I needed it. Again my experience in Zambia helped me out. I guess we North Americans and our "rat race," rush-rush-rush lifestyle are not accustomed to long sermons.

I began to retell the biblical story and to make comments as I went along. I asked questions to generate discussion. The discussion became a little heated when one woman responded to my statement that this woman was the first evangelist, when she went into the city and told the people about Jesus.

"You see, we women are just as important as you men are. We were the first evangelist; we're the ones Jesus first appeared to after his resurrection; we're the ones who helped to support his ministry with our own money. You macho men had better listen up. We women can be and are leaders in the church."

As the evening moved on, I came to realize that both Guillermo and I had joined the circle of people and were not standing behind the lectern. On the way back to the seminary, Guillermo asked me, "How did you know to give that kind of sermon and not preach as you do in the United States?"

Since we had not had time to talk much, he did not know this was the last two weeks of a ten-week travel/study in Mexico and Central America. He also did not know I had lived and preached in Zambia for three years.

"First, there was no way I could get up and talk even on the whole Bible for an hour without some preparation beforehand," I said. "Second, I knew from my time this summer with BCC and with village churches in Zambia that a dialogue sermon in a small, informal group setting was better. And third, I like to do it that way because I learn so much from the people. The reason I am here is to learn from the people. My preaching for an hour—no one was going to learn anything."

"Well I am not sure of that, but the people there think you are great. They have asked me to invite you back on Wednesday night and they want you to lead them again."

I was glad. I wanted to learn from them.

CONCLUSION

As the people in Latin America seek liberation of their lives, they find a liberation of their faith. They find that they are one in the same. Women have taken a lead in this liberation of their faith. For the most part, men write about liberation in books (see the bibliography), but at the grassroots level it is women who are seeking ways to free themselves and their families from oppression. Women suffer double and triple oppressions and they want freedom—from the oppression of rulers, where women have been dominated by unjust laws; from oppression in the church, where women have been dominated by the male hierarchy; from oppression in the marketplace, where women have been dominated by economic bureaucracy; from oppression in the family, where women have been dominated by their fathers, husbands, and son. This will come only after they have liberated themselves. Their faith, lived and expressed through Liberation Theology, has given them a way to a liberated life.

21

The Church Rules on Sexuality: Stories from the United States

The two women who share their stories below know each other, and there are places where their stories come together. Both are graduates of San Francisco Theological Seminary (SFTS). Lisa speaks of Janie, and Janie tells of when their cases were both before the General Assembly Church courts.[1] Both women are Presbyterian; Lisa is not ordained but Janie is. Their stories could be the stories of women in any of the churches in this country, where lesbians and gay men are not allowed to follow God's call to be in ministry through the church.

WILL SHE EVER BE ORDAINED

"Lisa, I remember you telling our small group at seminary that you were a lesbian," I began. "I felt so trusted that you would share that with us. As we got to know each other over the years and even shared a pulpit once, I have learned bits and pieces of your story. It has been five years since we graduated, so bring me up to date and fill me in on your life as a lesbian, called by God to serve."

Lisa and I were fellow students at San Francisco Theological Seminary from 1985-1989. Our senior year, Lisa was awarded both the Alumni/ae Fellowship and the David Esler Award in Homiletics at graduation. The first thing that amazed me about this outstanding woman was her mobility. Lisa is blind, but that never slowed her down. Once she had traveled an area, we would not see her white cane. With her sense of humor, she would have given any stand-up comics at the San Francisco Comedy Club a run for their money. Her keen mind and quick wit endeared her, not only to the seminary community but to the Bay Area. Here is your opportunity to begin to know this woman of faith. Listen to her story.

"I came out as a lesbian at the age of twenty, to some of my friends. By that time, I had fallen in love numerous times with other women. By the time I got to college, I had to begin to admit to myself just what these feelings meant for me.

"I had planned to continue on to seminary after I finished college. So in my senior year at college, I applied to several schools and decided on San Francisco Theological Seminary. I wasn't sure then what it would mean to pursue a career in the church as a lesbian woman, but going to seminary seemed the only path for me to follow.

"As I entered seminary at age twenty-one, I thought I could live a 'closeted' life. The church, along with other institutions, sets a 'trap' for lesbians and gay men. You can pursue a call and betray your identity, or you can live openly and sacrifice your 'call.' As I began seminary, I thought it would be possible to live the double life that the closet demands."

"Lisa, there were several gay men and lesbians at seminary, many of them in our own class. Was this group supportive for you as you thought of coming out, or were you closeted to them also?"

"We seemed to know who was homosexual, but that first year we didn't talk much together. By the time we graduated, we were much more supportive of each other. I think we all were being more cautious to begin with.

"As I became a part of the lesbian and gay community, my doubts about the closet grew. I moved to the Bay Area in 1985—a time when AIDS was ravaging the gay community. 'Silent death' was a familiar slogan among AIDS activists. I came to know that those of us who witnessed the deaths of our brothers had to tell their stories—and our own. I began to understand that the closet was a kind of privilege that had to be given up in the face of such a crisis."

"The AIDS crisis touched many of us," I agreed, "because of the large community of gay men and lesbians in the Bay Area. If for no other reason than hearing about it through the news media. I know I was aware of the Castro District in San Francisco—a friend took me there in 1975 to meet some of his friends. I remember wondering how people could hate the gay community when there was so much suffering and pain."

"It wasn't just the terrible tragedy of the AIDS crisis that brought me out of the closet," Lisa continued. "I gained a tremendous pride in the lesbian and gay community—I was deeply proud of the way we cared for each other. Also, I was proud and moved by the women and men who were out of the closet risking their reputations, their careers, their lives, in order that the world might be a safer and more just place for other lesbians, gay men, and bisexuals—a safer and more just place for me."

"Lisa, I remember you have a sister. There are just the two of you, right?"

"Yes. Did you know I am an aunt now? I love it."

"I think I remember when you went home to tell your family. What was that like?" I asked

"It was in 1988. You and I were living in the same seminary apartment building when I came out to my family. This was the greatest hurdle for me, and probably the most important step in my taking responsibility for my own life. I came to know that in the long run I hurt myself and my family more by not being fully myself."

"While still in seminary you took a massage therapist course. I thought, *Lisa is doing something that she has always wanted to do.* I had to study so hard that I hardly had time for anything but the books. I was envious of you. Was that part of your planning or was it just for the fun of it?" I asked.

"Knowing that I was no longer willing to live in the closet, I took the massage therapist course so I would have a fallback career. In 1989, when we graduated from SFTS, I was no longer willing to live in the closet. I fled to the other end of the 'trap'—I decided I wouldn't pursue a call to ordained ministry. Instead, I began a career as a massage therapist. Today, I continue to work in massage, and in many ways it is work that has brought me back to a deep and real faith."

"Our lives were not as connected after graduation. I knew you were out of the closet, but I was not sure what was happening in your life. Bring me up to date?" I asked.

"In 1990 two lesbian women, Ruth Frost and Phylis Zelhart, and one gay man, Jeff Johnson, were ordained 'irregularly' in the Lutheran Church. The two small churches that called them to be their pastors risked sanction and disciplinary action by the larger denomination, but they believed that the Lutheran Church's ban on ordaining lesbians and gay men was wrong.

"The example set by Phylis and Ruth meant a lot to me. I realized that by not challenging the church directly on its stand against the ordination of lesbians and gay men, I was tacitly allowing it to continue.

"That same year, my candidate's committee wrote to me saying that it was time to move forward with my candidacy—I had completed all the requirements and was ready to go through the interview process to be certified as ready to seek a call to ordained ministry. I knew what I needed to do. I wrote the committee and told them I couldn't continue in the process without letting them know that I was a lesbian. I guessed that they would move to have my name withdrawn as a candidate, but I wanted first, to be open, and second, for the committee, at least, to have a person and not just an issue to deal with.

"I met with the committee and they decided not to have my name withdrawn. Instead, they recommended to presbytery that I should be certified in November of 1991.

"I won't go into all the reasoning behind their decision, or the debate at presbytery, which ended with a vote to certify me as ready to seek a call. What is more important is that in that process I took hold of a sense of calling. I realized that I couldn't give up on the church, and I felt at times as though I had an almost palpable sense of being led. I felt called simply to be who I am, to be proud and happy in that, and from that I would find my way and my work."

"Lisa, I know you have been active in the gay community both inside and outside the church. What are you doing now?"

"Now I direct a project called Witness For Reconciliation,[2] which works mostly with Presbyterian churches in the Bay Area as they shape a dialogue around the question of ordination for lesbians and gay men."

"Is this a project under the Presbytery of San Francisco?"

"No, it is out of the Noe Valley Ministry. You know that church and its ministry is in the heart of the Castro District, the gay community in San Francisco. Several of the presbytery committees support my work, but I have not gone to the presbytery yet. I continue to be healthily wary of the church. I believe Audre Lorde's admonishment that the master's tools won't dismantle the master's house. We can easily delude ourselves into believing that we can work from within the structure to change it. Even so, I feel as though I have been given this path, and that it's my responsibility simply to be faithful in staying on it; I believe that when the path turns in a new direction, I'll know it."

"As a member of the session at St. John's there in Berkeley," I reflected, "when we went through the process of determining if we would become a 'More Light Church,'[3] I was aware that this was an issue that even liberal congregations, such as St. John's, had to deal with cautiously, with time and in-depth study, prayer, and listening. There are only, what, two or three 'More Light Churches' in the presbytery? How do you relate to them and feel about their support?"

"I know that those congregations are there and they have taken a risk in becoming supporting churches. They are part of the 'cloud of witnesses' and a link in a long line of supporters. There have been a lot of people, lesbians, gay men, and others, who have risked a lot in order that I might have more freedom. I know that the only way to repay them is by seeking to make the way easier for those who follow me.

"A friend of mine, Lindsay Biddle, a straight woman deeply dedicated to working for justice for lesbians, gay men, bisexuals, and transsexuals in the church, commented once that the real church isn't what happens when the good old boys get together and make their decisions. Mostly, the real church happens among women. People like Janie Spahr simply go out and speak to people, touching their lives and changing them. Certainly there are men in this real church too, but they aren't ruled by the patriarchy."

"Lisa, what is your hope for the future of lesbians and gay men in the Presbyterian Church?"

"I'm not sure that the Presbyterian Church will vote to allow the ordination of gay men and lesbians in my lifetime, but I believe that the church will change, or it will die. Meanwhile, I'm happy to be doing the work that I've been given."

IT FEELS SO RIGHT BUT THEY CALLED IT BAD

"Janie, first I would like for you to talk about your life as a girl and some of your first memories of your knowing that you were a lesbian."

"I am a twin. It was very easy for me to communicate with others, since I had done it through the womb and all of my life. Ever since I was a child I have been able to feel God and know God from deep within myself. I just knew I loved people and I loved God. When I was about eight years old, there was a missionary who spoke at our church. He said, 'If I were younger I would work with the poor.' I thought he was talking to me and I said to myself, 'I am young and I could do that.'

"By the time I was fourteen I knew I was to be in ministry. At the same time I knew where my deepest feelings were. My deepest feelings were for my friends. I had boyfriends, but it was in my feeling for my friends that I felt God deep inside of me. I did not know what that feeling meant at that time."

"What was your first experience with these feelings in relation to how the straight community viewed the gay community?" I asked.

"When I went away to prep school at fourteen I remember going into a café with some of the girls and one of them pointed to two women. The girls were saying the women were 'queers,' they were dirty, and they were bad. I felt a connection with the two women and wondered if the deep feelings I had were the same; was I that too? Was I dirty? Was I bad?

"Although I was Presbyterian I visited a Catholic church many times and lit candle after candle. I asked God if this feels so good and so right, how come people are saying that it is bad? I asked God to help me to get over whatever these feelings were.

"I remember how people talked about people labeled 'queer' and I knew that I had better keep these feelings to myself."

"Janie, did you have boyfriends? Did you date? Were you able to talk with any of your girlfriends about your feelings?

"Yes, I had boyfriends. I had one girlfriend I shared my feelings with. She had told me about her boyfriends, so I thought I could share my thoughts with her. Her response was, 'Janie, that is awful!' I knew then that I had better be careful about what I said. This made me very sad, because I started to separate myself from both my sexuality and my spirituality. I began to die within myself."

"Had you told your twin sister about your feelings?" I asked.

"I told my twin and my father and mother. They were in such shock that we didn't talk about it again. I knew they loved me; they just did not understand, so I left it alone. I thought, I will get over it."

"You have said several times that you thought you would get over it, that you were buying into that myth. Was there ever any time when the idea that you would get over it was supported by other people?"

"When I was in college, I felt being drawn to my friends, and it frightened me. I couldn't understand why something that felt so good in the God place, as I call it, inside of me, could still not be right. I was buying into what people were saying. When I was a senior in college, I wrote an autobiography. I got a note from our professor, a psychologist, who asked me to come and see him. He told me, 'Don't worry, you will get over this, it is just a stage.' I believed him because I believed that he must know."

"Did you meet your husband Jim in college?"

"Yes, he asked me to marry him in my senior year. I talked with him about my feelings and what the psychologist had said, that I would get over this, it was just a stage. Jim also knew that I wanted to go to seminary. I had kept that deep feeling for God all the way through this struggle with my sexuality. Jim was one of the few men I had dated who understood my goal of going to seminary and was willing to consider being a pastor's spouse."

Knowing Janie is no longer in her marriage relationship with Jim, I asked her, "When did you begin to realize in your marriage that your lesbian feelings were not going to go away?"

"I think it was about five years into the marriage. I was serving a church in Pittsburgh, Pennsylvania, where this incredible African American woman, Wanda Graham Harris, was my associate. She taught me so much in the year I was there. She taught me how to pray and to preach. She said, 'When you pray, sit there with your hands open. As though you will be receiving something.' The more I learned from Wanda about God in the intimacy, the more I got in touch with myself. This was frightening to me. Jim and I talked about my feelings and our marriage. I still was not sure what words to put to the feelings. Queer was the word used. Queer, I thought, meant a woman who wanted to be a man, and I knew that was not what I was feeling. All Jim and I knew was the terrible mythology around being lesbian or gay.

"We had moved back to the San Francisco Bay Area where I was youth minister in a church. About this time Jim read the book by Don Clark, *Loving Someone Gay*,[4] and suggested I read it. I was afraid to read the book. It was about that time the Presbyterian Church was studying the issue of homosexuality in the church, 1976–1978. I was invited to speak to our Presbytery Task Force about women in ministry. The question was posed whether there was a correlation between the oppression of women and the oppression of lesbian and gay people.

"Just before I was to speak, Ellen Barrett, the first ordained Episcopal lesbian priest and Bill Johnson, an ordained gay minister of the United Church of Christ, spoke. As they told their story, I knew it was my story. After the meeting I went right home and told Jim about the meeting. We cried and cried. We cried out of the relief we felt. Because when you love someone deeply and you are not meeting in the deepest place, there is this sense of lose, of sadness.

"That night at the supper table, Jim said, 'Tell the boys, Mom, what has been going on today, and the wonderful news you have to tell them about yourself.' They were five and seven years old. The boys were just great. One said, 'Mommy, you love people and that's what's most important.' The other one said, 'Isn't this great, Mom, let's tell the church.' We told them we didn't think the church would be as excited as we were. My support from my family was phenomenal."

"I understand you worked for the Council of Oakland Presbyterian Churches. Tell me about what happened there," I said.

"I had separated from Jim and was living with a woman I had met. We had our children with us, my two and her two. I had also left the congregation I had been working for and have accepted the call to the Council. There was a called meeting of the Council of Oakland Presbyterian Churches. They told me they were very happy with my work. I said to them, 'If you love my work and you love what I am doing, will someone say what's going on here so that we can hear it out loud. What is the problem for me to continue my work?'

"Finally someone said out loud, 'Janie, it is because you are a lesbian.' Following that meeting, it all came out to the church."

"Did you leave the ministry in the Presbyterian Church at that time?" I asked.

"Yes, I was called by the Metropolitan Christian Church (MCC)—a predominantly lesbian and gay church, in San Francisco, where I served for two and a half years. While I was there, I was nurtured and grew in my faith and in my understanding of myself as a lesbian woman."

"When did you return to ministry in the Presbyterian Church?"

"In 1982, I became the director of the Ministry of Light in Marin Country, in the North Bay Area. There were people in the Presbyterian Church who were upset that I was not in the Presbyterian denomination per se any more. Friends began looking for ways that I could do ministry within the church. That is when we started the Ministry of Light. I worked with lesbian, gay, bisexual, and transsexual persons, and with persons with HIV/AIDS. I also became involved with Presbyterians for Lesbian and Gay Concerns," Janie explained.

"Over the last several years, since 1991, you have been involved in the process of being called by the Downtown United Presbyterian Church in Rochester, New York. Tell me about that," I asked.

"It was in November of 1991 that I was called to candidate for a co-pastor position at the Downtown Church. Coni, my partner, and I went back to visit. It was an exciting and thoughtful time for the church and for us. The presbytery also confirmed my call, but there were ten churches out of the seventy-six, that filed charges against the Downtown Church for calling a lesbian minister. The synod also ruled in our favor, but then it went to the General Assembly Permanent Judicial Commission of the church. By this time it was Halloween, 1992. Lisa Larges, the finest and best preacher I have ever heard, and my case were heard at the same time. We were hoping for two yeses. Because our presbyteries and one synod had ruled in our favor, we felt that the highest church court might also. But they didn't.

"I returned to my work at the Ministry of Light, which was renamed, in 1992, Spectrum Center for Lesbian, Gay, and Bisexual Concerns. But the Downtown Church was not giving up on our covenant together. They asked me if I would be willing to serve as an evangelist and travel around the country talking about an inclusive church, talking about sexuality and spirituality, and personalizing this issue. Since March of 1993, I have been serving as an evangelist, spreading the good news about how God is part of each of us in both our sexuality and our spirituality."

CONCLUSION

There is so much more to learn from each of these women. Although I have known each of them for years, hearing their stories again in this way has caused me to look deeper into myself. As Janie says, "When you know your deepest self, you can love yourself and love others." Knowing ourselves—sexually—and loving ourselves—spiritually—for these two women and for all women is a gift to ourselves from our God, whatever name we use.

22

Still Moving Forward

If the world was listening in the fall of 1995, they heard that the women are still moving forward. At their Fourth UN World Conference on Women (Conference) and the NGO Forum in China, the women of the world spoke it loud and clear that they are not turning back.

Gertrude Mongella, Secretary-General of the Fourth UN World Conference on Women, stated in her address to the Conference, "We must watch out for conservative or backward-looking elements which want to keep the woman in a place where she has always been. A revolution has begun. There can be no spectators, no sideliners, no abstainers, for this is a crucial social agenda that affects all humanity." This was the call for men to join women. Over the last twenty years the women of the world have been gaining in self-confidence, cooperative leadership skills, community development, and consensus building. They know that the problems they face each day cannot be solved by them alone. They realize that men play a part in the problems. Therefore the women of the world are calling on men—in their families, their communities, their nations, and the world—to join them in addressing the problems.

"Cementing the partnership of women and men is critical," said Mongella. "Women have all along struggled with their menfolk for the abolition of slavery, the liberation of countries from colonialism, the dismantling of apartheid and the struggle for peace. It is now the turn of men to join women in their struggle for equality."

In struggling for equality there are twelve critical areas of concern that were discussed by both the women who met at the UN Conference in Beijing and at the NGO Forum in Huairou. These twelve critical areas of concern are: poverty, education, health, violence against women, effects of armed conflict, economic structures and policies, inequality of men and women in decision making, gender equality, women's rights, media, environment, and girl child.

"Looking at The World through Women's Eyes" was an appropriate slogan for the NGO Forum, because one of the main thrusts that came out of the workshops, discussions, and networking was that issues need to be defined from a woman's perspective and a woman's values. For far too long women's concerns have been defined by men from their perspective and values. A good example of this is the defining of reproductive health, which men have for the most part defined it as pre- and postnatal care. Women are saying that definition is too narrow, that it must be redefined to include the complete life span of a female, from conception to death. As one woman from Uganda said in discussing sex education as part of reproductive health, "We have to take out that word 'sex' which the men put in and call it what it is, 'health education.' We want our children, both girls and boys, to know about their bodies, how they function, and how to care for them. Who can object to that? Let's get rid of the word 'sex,' get it out of here and be on about educating our children."

The "Platform of Action," which was accepted unanimously by the Conference, set forth strategic objectives for each of the twelve critical areas of concern as well as actions to be taken by all levels of government and NGOs. Unfortunately, this document is not a binding treaty, rather it is a set of guidelines for the advancement of women into the Twenty-first century. Through discussion and consensus the delegates arrived at their unanimous vote with, alas, some restrictions placed by some countries. The leadership of the Conference as well as the attenders of the NGO Forum realize that the work begins when all of the women return to their homes. If there is to be continued growth it will come from the grassroots as the "Platform of Action" is carry out.

Hillary Rodham Clinton, one of thirty first ladies to attend both the Conference and the NGO Forum, lifted up the cry of women around the world when she forcefully stated that "women's rights are human rights and human rights are women's rights." This cry was first heard at the UN Conference on Human Rights held in Austria in 1993. The progress made in 1993 carried over and became the underlying concern for the women meeting in China. These rights included—equal treatment before the law and laws that respected women's rights, including inheritance laws; the freedom to live in a nonviolent world, be it in the family, community, or nation; a woman's right to decide freely on the number and spacing of the children she bears; that unpaid work of women be assigned a value when figuring both Gross National Product (GNP) and Gross Domestic Product (GDP); the right to credit; opportunity in education; health care.

The women meeting in China spoke out for the family when they reminded their sisters that when you address issues affecting women you are addressing issues related to the family, because it is the women of the world who are the nurturers and caregivers in families. They also pointed out that the nuclear family of father, mother, and children is now in the minority. They were also quick to point regardless if there is a father in the family it is still the mother's responsibility to be the one who passes on the culture and traditions. As one woman from Nigeria said, "We want to keep those cultural traditions that support and sustain our families, but we must identify those traditions that oppress women and therefore oppress the family. Not everything we do today is right and good for the family, and not every tradition that has been passed down is good. We as women must identify them and work to alleviate them."

We have read stories of how women have identified problems in their lives and, by working together, empowered themselves and their sisters. The women that met in China know these same problems and celebrated the progress that has been made over the last twenty years. In their celebration they also set new goals for the new century. Yet they knew that all would be for naught if they did not return to their homes and begin to carry out the "Platform of Action." They knew that they have to work with men in addressing the twelve critical areas of concern. They knew that they had to change definitions and truly bring the world to look at itself through the eyes of women. They would have agreed that it is true for their country what my friend Emily claimed for Zambia when she said, "If you want to know Zambia, get to know the women. The problems we face each day are the real problems of this country. The joys we have, the life we celebrate, are the joys and life of Zambia."

Notes

PREFACE

1. Frank Waters, *The Earp Brothers of Tombstone* (New York: Bramhall House, 1940), p. 8.

2. Elisabeth Schussler Fiorenza, *In Memory of Her* (New York: Crossroad, 1985), p. 132.

1. WOMEN EMPOWERING WOMEN

1. Kathleen Fischer, *Women at the Well* (New York: Paulist Press, 1988), p. 196.

2. It is very common for women to have dresses made out of cloth that makes a statement. I saw dresses with President Kaunda's picture on the cloth and with the flag or symbols and slogans. During campaigning, candidates would have cloth printed with their picture and slogan and women would make dresses of the cloth. We have T-shirts, they have dresses.

3. "Self-reliance and autonomy do not mean isolation of the individual, or individualism, but rather, autonomy and self-reliance linked to the family and society." Devaki Jain, "Gandhian Contributions toward a Feminist Ethic," in *Speaking of Faith: Global Perspective on Women Religion and Social Change*, ed. Diana L. Eck and Devaki Jain (Philadelphia: New Society Publishers, 1987), p. 277.

4. Ibid., p. 286–87.

5. Ibid., p. 278.

6. Ibid., p. 287.

7. Nawal el Saadawi, "Toward Women's Power, Nationally and Internationally," in *Speaking of Faith: Global Perspective on Women Religion and Social Change*,

eds. Diana L. Eck and Devaki Jain (Philadelphia: New Society Publishers, 1987), p. 269.

8. Diana L. Eck and Devaki Jain, "Building a Common Foundation For Social Change: Introduction," in *Speaking of Faith: Global Perspective on Women Religion and Social Change*, eds. Diana L. Eck and Devaki Jain (Philadelphia: New Society Publishers, 1987), p. 249.

2. HOW IT ALL WORKS

1. The resources for this section are many: newspapers, reports from UN agencies, the World Bank and International Monetary Fund (IMF), and nongovernmental agencies. Following is a list of sources on the history of global economic development: Donald L. Barlet and James B. Steele, *America: What Went Wrong?* (Kansas City, MO: Andrews and McMeel, 1992); Richard J. Barnet and Ronald E. Muller, *Global Reach: The Power of the Multinational Corporations*, (New York: Simon and Schuster, 1974); John Cavanagh, et al., eds., *Trading Freedom: How Free Trade Affects Our Lives, Work, and Environment* (San Francisco: The Institute for Food and Development Policy, 1992); John Cavanagh, et al., eds., *From Debt to Development: Alternatives to the International Debt Crisis* (Washington, DC: The Institute for Policy Studies, 1985); Susan George, *A Fate Worse Than Debt: The World Financial Crisis and the Poor*, (New York: Grove Press, 1988); Frances Moore Lappe and Joseph Collins, *World Hunger: Twelve Myths*, (New York: Grove Press, 1986); Jack Nelson-Pallmeyer, *Brave New World Order* (Maryknoll, NY: Orbis Books, 1992); Walter L. Owensby, *Economics for Prophets: A Primer on Concepts, Realities, and Values in Our Economic System* (Grand Rapids, MI: William B. Eerdmans Publishing, 1988); George Ann Potter, *Dialogue on Debt: Alternative Analyses and Solutions* (Washington, DC: The Center of Concern, 1988).

2. Oscar A. Romero, *Voice of the Voiceless* (Maryknoll, NY: Orbis Books, 1985), p. 188.

3. Richard J. Barnet and Ronald E. Muller, *Global Reach: The Power of the Multinational Corporations* (New York: Simon and Schuster, 1974), p. 153.

4. Ibid., pp. 152–53.

5. "Free-Trade Zones," sometimes also called export-processing zones, are areas in many third world countries where TLCs can set up business with few taxes, safety regulations, or environment controls. The host country provides cheap labor.

6. Barnet and Muller, p. 155.

7. Ibid., chapter 2 "From Globaloney to the Global Shopping Center."

8. Ibid., p. 149.

9. Ibid.

10. Ibid., p. 150.

11. Jack Nelson-Pallmeyer, *Brave New World Order* (Maryknoll, NY: Orbis Books, 1992), p. 9, as quoted in Ecumenical Coalition for Economic Justice,

Recolonization or Liberation: The Bonds of Structural Adjustment and Struggles for Emancipation (Toronto, Canada: Ecumenical Coalition for Economic Justice, 1990), p. 6.

12. *Nshima* is the staple food in Zambia. It is made out of white corn meal and is some what like corn meal mush.

3. WORKING TOGETHER: STORIES FROM AFRICA

1. Sharon Capeling-Alakija, *Annual Report 1990 United Nations Development Fund for Women,* (New York: UNIFEM, 1991), p. 14.

2. Heifer Project International is an nongovernmental organization (NGO) with headquarters in Little Rock, Arkansas. It provides breeding livestock and education and training in the care of the livestock to persons of low income to give them a hand-up. The person has to agree to give the first offspring to a neighbor and that neighbor to another and so on. The livestock ranges from heifers to bees, from chicks to rabbits, from goats to pigs. The address is Heifer Project International, P.O. Box 808, 1015 South Louisiana, Little Rock, AK, 72203, phone: 501-376-6836.

4. WOMEN'S WORK IS NEVER ENDING: STORIES FROM ASIA

1. Sergy Floro and Nana Luz, *Sourcebook on Philippine Women in Struggle* (Berkeley, CA: Philippine Resource Center, 1985), p. 39.

2. Ibid., p. 60.

3. Ibid., p. 138.

5. WORK THAT OPPRESSES: STORIES FROM LATIN AMERICA

1. "Green Revolution was introduced in the 1950s. It is a policy of intensifying food production through developing hybrid, high-yield seed varieties demanded extensive irrigation and increased mechanization, as well as the use of fertilizers and pesticides." Irene Dankelman and Joan Davidson, *Women and Environment in the Third World: Alliance for the Future* (London: Earthscan Publications Ltd, 1988), pp. 9-10.

2. Dankelman and Davidson, p. 120.

3. Ibid., pp. 120, 148-49.

4. A shelter built of branches, or in this case of cane stalks.

5. Basic Christian Communities (BCC's) are small groups of Christians who come together to study the Bible and reflect on how the Bible is relevant to their daily lives and what kind of life God and Jesus wants them to live. These groups are found in all countries in Latin America and have spread to other countries.

6. Peasant farmers both female and male.

7. Elvia Alvarado, with Medea Benjamin, ed., *Don't Be Afraid, Gringo: The Story of Elvia Alvarado* (San Francisco: Food First, 1987).

6. WOMEN AND UNIONS: STORIES FROM THE UNITED STATES

1. "AIWA Celebrates Its 1st Decade," *The Newsletter of Asian Immigrant Women Advocates,* June 1994, Vol. 10, No. 2, p. 3, col. 2.

2. *Immigrant Women Speak Out: On Garment Industry Abuse* (Oakland, CA: Asian Immigrant Women Advocates, 1993), p. 3.

3. Ibid., p. 2.

4. *Maquiladoras* are factories along the Mexico-United States border where companies from other countries, the majority from the United States, have moved a large part of the production. These factories have poor health standards, low wages, and pollute the soil, water, and air, thus causing multiple health problems for the workers.

5. Sarah Henry, "Labor & Lace," *San Francisco Chronicle,* September 5, 1993, Sec. This World, p. 9, col. 1.

6. Cecilia Rodriguez, *Linking Our Struggles,* The Newsletter of Asian Immigrant Women Advocates, June 1994, Vol. 10, No. 2, p. 2, col. 2.

7. Wing Lam, "Editorial: Workers' Centers and the New Labor Movement," *CSWA News: The Voice of Chinese American Workers,* Summer 1994, Vol. 4, Issue 1, p. 6.

8. Robert B. Reich, Secretary of Labor, *News Release* (Washington, DC: U.S. Department of Labor, March 18, 1996).

7. VOTING IS NOT ENOUGH

1. Linda Grant DePauw, *Founding Mothers: Women in America in the Revolutionary Era* (Boston: Houghton Mifflin, 1975), p. 203.

2. Ibid., p. xi.

3. Miriam Gurko, *The Ladies of Seneca Falls: The Birth of the Woman's Rights Movement* (New York: Schocken Books, 1976), p. 5.

4. Naomi Wolf, *Fire with Fire: The New Female Power and How to Use It.* (New York: Fawcett Columbine, 1994).

5. Ibid., p. 22.

6. Ibid., p. 23.

7. Kumari Jayawardena, *Feminism and Nationalism in the Third World* (London: Zed Books, 1986), p. ix.

8. Ibid.

9. Ibid., p. 8.

10. Hans Morgenthau, *Politics Among Nations: The Struggle for Power and Peace* 5th rev. ed. (New York: Alfred Knopf, 1973), pp. 4–15, as quoted by J. Ann Tickner, "Hans Morgenthau's Principles of Political Realism: A Feminist Reformulation," in *Gender and International Relations,* eds. Rebecca Grant and Kathleen Newland (Bloomington, IN: Indiana University Press, 1991), p. 29.

11. Ibid., p. 36.

12. Ibid., p. 37.

13. The term "conscientization" refers to learning to perceive social, political, and economic contradictions and to take action against the oppressive elements of reality. See Paulo Freire, *Pedagogy of the Oppressed* (New York: Continuum, 1986), p. 19.

14. Levi Oracion, *Ideologies and People's Struggles for Justice, Freedom, and Peace* (Geneva, Switzerland: World Council of Churches, 1988), p. 5.

15. Ibid., p. 3.

16. Steven Shrybman, "Selling the Environment Short," in *Trading Freedom: How Free Trade Affects Our Lives, Work, and Environment*, eds. John Cavanagh, John Gershman, Karen Baker, and Gretchen Helmke (San Francisco: The Institute for Food and Development Policy, 1992), p. 40.

17. Joyce Gelb and Marian Lief Palley, *Women and Public Policies* (Princeton, NJ: Princeton University Press, 1982), p. 20.

8. WOMEN OF COURAGE: STORIES FROM AFRICA

1. Mervate F. Hatem, "The Paradoxes of State Feminism in Egypt," *Women and Politices Worldwide*, eds. Barbara J. Nelson and Najma Chowdhury (New Haven, CT: Yale University Press, 1994), p. 234.

2. Nawal el Saadawi, "Egypt: When a Woman Rebels . . . ," in *Sisterhood Is Global*, ed. Robin Morgan (Garden City, NY: Anchor Press/Doubleday, 1984), p. 200.

3. Nawal el Saadawi, "Toward Women's Power, Nationally and Internationally," in *Speaking of Faith: Global Perspective on Women Religion and Social Change*, eds. Diana L. Eck and Devaki Jain (Philadelphia: New Society Publishers, 1987), p. 269.

4. Ibid., p. 270.

5. Katherine Roth, "An Egyptian Feminist's Fight to Protect Hard-Won Gains," *San Francisco Chronicle*, September 23, 1991, Sec. Briefing.

6. Ibid.

7. Saadawi, "Toward Women's Power, Nationally and Internationally," in *Speaking of Faith: Global Perspective on Women Religion and Social Change*, eds. Eck and Jain, p. 274.

8. The African National Congress had its exiled headquarters in Zambia until the ban was lifted after the release from prison of its leader Nelson Mandela.

9. This is a term used in many parts of eastern and southern Africa when asking a person if you might walk part way with them. When you leave a friend's home they would escort you part of the way to your home.

10. *Apartheid Inside Outside* (Amsterdam: Roeland Kerbosch Film Produksie, 1978), as quoted in *Women Under Apartheid* (London: International Defence and Aid Fund for Southern Africa, 1981), p. 75.

11. Link No. 32 (Environmental and Development Agency, 1982), p. 23, quoted in Jane Barrett and others, *South African Women On The Move* (London: Zed Books, 1985), pp. 205–06.

9. WOMEN CROSSING THE LINE FOR PEACE: STORIES FROM ASIA

1. Sam Keen, *Faces of the Enemy: Reflections of the Hostile Imagination* (San Francisco: Harper & Row, 1986), p. 172.

2. Ibid., p. 172.

3. Ibid., p. 11.

4. A song from Richard Rodgers and Oscar Hammerstein's, *South Pacific*, 1949.

5. Jean Zaru has lived her entire life in Ramallah (originally Palestine, and since 1967 a part of the militarily occupied West Bank). She is an Arab, a Quaker, and a pacifist. She has been a member of the Central Committee of the World Council of Churches and is a vice president of the World YWCA.

6. Pacific Southwest Conference on World Christian Mission, Asilomar, CA, 1992.

7. On May 8, 1984, Benjamin M. Weir was kidnapped by Shiite Muslim extremists just outside his apartment in West Beirut, Lebanon, while his wife Carol looked on. Ben with his wife had been Presbyterian missionaries for thirty-one years in Lebanon. After sixteen months and seven days, Ben was released on September 15, 1985.

8. Sergy Floro and Nana Luz, eds., *Sourcebook on Philippine Women in Struggle*, (Berkeley, CA: Philippine Resource Center, 1985), p. 133.

10. WOMEN AND REVOLUTION: STORIES FROM LATIN AMERICA AND THE CARIBBEAN

1. With the collapse of the Soviet Union and the withdrawal of the financial support and the market for their products Cuba has been in recession.

2. Frente Farabundo Marti para la Liberacion Nacional. They are also called the guerrillas.

11. WORKING FOR PEACE IN MANY WAYS: STORIES FROM THE UNITED STATES

1. I had known of the Fellowship of the Least Coin since it became a part of the Presbyterian women's prayer life in 1957. My mother, treasurer for her women's group, told me how each time they met they would pray for women in other countries and then each would give a penny—our least coin—to symbolize the sharing of all women around the world.

2. He (Jesus) sat down opposite the treasury and watched the crowd putting money into the treasury. Many rich people put in large sums. A poor widow came and put in two small copper coins, which are worth a penny. Then he called his disciples and said to them, "Truly I tell you, this poor widow has put in more than all those who are contributing to the treasury. For all of them have contributed out of their abundance; but she out of her poverty has put in everything she had, all she had to live on." Mark 12:41–44, New Revised Standard Version.

3. Shirin Samuel, *Fellowship of the Least Coin: Global Movement of Prayer for Peace, Justice, and Reconciliation* (Multan, Pakistan: Fellowship of the Least Coin, n.d.), pp. 3–4.

4. Most people refer to using nonviolence to obstruct the entrance and to being arrested as civil disobedience. Many of us use the term "moral obedience" because we feel we are being obedient to a higher moral calling.

5. You can find Sadako's story in Eleanor Coerr, *Sadako* (New York: G.P. Putnam's Sons, 1993).

12. VIOLENCE AGAINST WOMEN

1. "Equal Rights For Women (and Girls)," *Women 2000*, No. 3, 1992, Vienna, Austria: Division for the Advancement of Women, Centre for Social Development and Humanitarian Affairs, 1992, p. 5.

2. The main source for the material regarding FGM has come from: UNICEF, *The Progress of Nations* (New York: UNICEF House, 1994) p. 35.

3. Peter Holden, Jurgen Horlemann, and Georg Friedrich Pfafflin, eds., *Tourism Prostitution Development: Documentation* (Bangkok, Thailand: Ecumenical Coalition on Third World Tourism, 1985), p. 1.

4. UNICEF, *The Progress of Nations*, p. 39.

5. Justice for Women Committee, *Myths and Facts about Rape and Battering* (Louisville, KY: Presbyterian Church (USA), n.d.), pp. 3–4.

6. National Victim Center and Crime Victims Research and Treatment Center, *Rape in America: A Report to the Nation* (Arlington, VA: National Victim Center, 1992), no page number.

7. Ibid., p. 6.

8. Ibid., p. 5.

9. Justice for Women, pp. 2–3.

10. Joan Zorza, *The Gender Bias Committee's Domestic Violence Study: Important Recommendations and First Steps* (Boston: Boston Bar J.4, 13, July/August 1989).

11. Patrick A. Langan and Christopher A. Innes, *Prevent Domestic Violence against Women* (Washington, DC: U.S. Department of Justice, 1986), p. 3.

12. Morgan, p. 8.

13. Ibid.

13. FEMALE GENITAL MUTILATION: STORIES FROM AFRICA

1. Nawal el Saadawi, *The Hidden Face of Eve: Women in the Arab World*, (London: Zed Books Ltd., 1980), p. 7.

2. Ibid., p. 40.

3. A *chtangy* is two meters of cloth used in many different ways such as: to tie a baby on your back, tie goods in it and carry on your head, tie around you to protect your clothing, to sit or lie on, to drape over a bush and sit under it in the shade, and even to use in dances.

4. Even though AIDS has swept through Africa and there is an upsurge in prostitution, both adult and child, women raised in the tribal traditions were taught that sexual intercourse was the wife's responsibility to her husband but the women were not to have pleasure or enjoyment from it. It was a service provided for the husband's needs. This is why women like Lois, Ruth, Leah, and Rachel were unaware that women can experience pleasure from sexual experiences.

14. CHILDREN ARE BECOMING THE CHOICE OF MEN: STORIES FROM ASIA

1. When the words "child" or "children" are used in reference to prostitution in this context they refer to girls unless otherwise stated. The majority of the child prostitutes are girls, some as young as eight and nine years of age.

2. Prawase Wasi, "Tourism and Child Prostitution," in *Caught in Modern Slavery: Tourism and Child Prostitution in Asia*, ed. Koson Srisang (Bangkok, Thailand: The Ecumenical Coalition on Third World Tourism, 1990), p. 26.

3. Ibid., p. 27.

4. ECPAT-USA, *West Coast Newsletter*, May 1993, p. 1. For information and data contact End Child Prostitution in Asian Tourism (ECPAT-WEST), P.O. Box 1142, Santa Monica, CA 90403-5784 (2210 Wilshire Blvd.), Fax: 310-829-9169; or ECPAT-USA, 475 Riverside Dr., Rm. 616, New York, NY 10115, 212-870-2074 or -2305, Fax: 212-870-2005.

5. The International Catholic Child Bureau in Geneva, Switzerland, has published a 200-page book, *The Sexual Exploitation of Children: Field Responses*. This is a collection of reports of forty-nine worldwide projects working on the issue of the rehabilitation of children who have been used as prostitutes. It supports the claims of the lack of support and recognition. This book can be ordered from ICCB, 65 rue de Lausanne, CH-1202, Geneva, Switzerland.

6. I met Yayori Matsui, a Japanese journalist, at the preview of the film. She told me she was doing some investigation on child prostitution. In her book, (Yayori Matsui, *Women's Asia,* [London: Zed Books Ltd., 1984]) she shares what she found while investigating both in Thailand and the Philippines. Her book is listed in the bibliography.

7. Kapok is a silky, cottonlike fiber that is in the long, wide, seed pod of the ceiba tree. The women gather the pods and strip the cotton out of the pods and separate the seeds from the cotton like fiber and sell both. The kapok is used for padding and the seeds for oil and meal. It is very similar to cotton except it does not mat together like cotton.

8. Thailand is one of the countries where cash crops are grown on large land holdings therefore smaller substances farmers are not able to sell their crops.

9. Matsui, p. 78.

15. MEN'S HONOR—WOMEN'S LIVES: STORIES FROM LATIN AMERICA

1. *Colonia* is a geographical area within a city or town. They vary in size but there is usually a feeling of community. The people in the *colonia* often work

together on projects for improvement and also celebrate together. Sometimes there is a church serving just one *colonia*, but usually several *colonias* make up a parish of the Catholic church.

2. It is a tradition that the boyfriend would give his girlfriend a bracelet or a watch instead of a ring when they were engaged.

17. WOMEN'S DEEP SPIRITUALITY

1. In purdah is to be kept in seclusion within the house. The women are not allowed to go out of the house or yard. If they do they have to be accompanied by a male relative.

2. Anthills in that part of Zambia could be as high as twenty to thirty feet with broad bases. Often times, the people would level off the top and build a hut on top.

18. EVIL DEATH SPIRIT: STORIES FROM AFRICA

1. These traditions that I am referring to are a part of the culture that includes religious beliefs. Traditional religious practices are often incorporated into the new religion that the person may acquire, be it Christianity or Islam. I also found second- and third-generation Christians who still accepted traditional customs.

2. I was a missionary teacher at Njase Girls Secondary School which was located about five kilometers from Choma, Zambia. This boarding school had about 600 students and 100 faculty, staff, workers, and their families. The school compound was enclosed by a high fence, and the faculty and top staff personnel lived within the school compound. What we would call streets they called roads. Single persons lived in duplexes and married persons lived in houses. The first term I was there, I shared a duplex with Elizabeth because of the housing shortage.

3. It did not matter what you ate with your tea, it was still called sweets. It might be a scone with or without jam, or it might be a biscuit—what we would call a cookie but more like tasteless cardboar—or it could be a piece of toast.

4. The "British" English word for any size truck. In this case a pick-up truck.

19. EXPRESSING THEIR SPIRITUALITY: STORIES FROM ASIA

1. I hope the women will forgive me for writing their stories after all. Their stories touched me and I hope will touch other women. When I was there, I did not know I would be sharing these women's stories with you.

2. *Ashram* is a community, sometimes in a retreat setting and sometimes a gathering of like-minded persons within a village or community. There is a common sharing of work, resources, and teaching by a leader or *guru*.

20. SPIRITUALITY IS THEIR LIBERATION:
STORIES FROM LATIN AMERICA

1. A delegate of the word is a person who works in the church and teaches Bible classes. The people are usually community leaders who help the people in whatever way they can. This term that is usually associated with the Roman Catholic church, but this BCC was part of the Presbyterian Church of Guatemala.

21. THE CHURCH RULES ON SEXUALITY:
STORIES FROM THE UNITED STATES

1. In the Presbyterian Church (USA), there are four levels of government and church courts: the session of the congregation; the presbytery, made up of a group of congregations in a specific geographical area; the synod, made up of a group of presbyteries in a specific geographical area; and the highest, the general assembly, which includes all the church members in the United States. There are representatives elected from each level for the higher levels. It is a representative form of church government.

2. Lisa's Witness For Reconciliation ministry has a traveling dramatic presentation by lesbians, gay men, and parents telling their stories. I attended a presentation one Sunday evening in Oakland, California. The Spirit was moving among us that evening.

3. The name "More Light Congregation" is used by the Presbyterian Church (USA) for those congregations that openly support lesbians and gay men. This support includes the ordination of both deacons and elders and the support of ordination of the word and sacrament (clergy). Some persons in the Presbyterian Church (USA) interpret this as going against church law. Most mainline churches have a designated name for congregations that openly support lesbians and gay men, for example United Church of Christ and Disciples of Christ have Open and Affirming Congregations, United Methodists have Reconciling Church.

4. Don Clark, *Loving Someone Gay* (New York: NAL-Dutton, 1978).

Selected Bibliography

WOMEN'S RESOURCE BOOKS

Bumiller, Elisabeth. *May You Be the Mother of a Hundred Sons: A Journey Among the Women of India*. New York: Fawcett Columbine, 1990.

Cantor, Dorothy W., and Toni Bernay. *Women in Power: The Secrets of Leadership*. Boston: Houghton Mifflin, 1992.

Cole, Johnnetta B., ed. *All American Women: Lines that Divide, Ties that Bind*. New York: Free Press, 1986.

Dankelman, Irene, and Joan Davidson. *Women and Environment in the Third World: Alliance for the Future*. London: Earthscan Publications, 1988.

Deckard, Barbara Sinclair. *The Women's Movement: Political, Socioeconomic, and Psychological Issues*. New York: Harper & Row, 1983.

DePauw, Linda Grant. *Founding Mothers: Women in America in the Revolutionary Era*. Boston: Houghton Mifflin, 1975.

Faludi, Susan. *Backlash: The Undeclared War Against American Women*. New York: Doubleday, 1991.

Fernea, Elizabeth Warnock, ed. *Women and the Family in the Middle East: New Voices of Change*. Austin: University of Texas Press, 1985.

Flexner, Eleanor. *Century of Struggle: The Women's Rights Movement in the United States*. New York: Atheneum, 1972.

Floro, Sergy, and Nana Luz. *Sourcebook on Philippine Women in Struggle*. Berkeley, CA: Philippine Resource Center, 1985.

Friedan, Betty. *The Feminine Mystique*. New York: Dell Publishing Co., 1963.

Gilligan, Carol. *In a Different Voice: Psychological Theory and Women's Development*. Cambridge: Harvard University Press, 1982.

168   Selected Bibliography

Gurko, Miriam. *The Ladies of Seneca Falls: The Birth of the Woman's Rights Movement.* New York: Schocken Books, 1976.

Jayawardena, Kumari. *Feminism and Nationalism in the Third World.* London: Zed Books, 1986.

Katz, Naomi, and Nancy Milton, eds. *Fragment from a Lost Diary and Other Stories: Women of Asia, Africa, and Latin America.* Boston: Beacon Press, 1973.

Kishwar, Madhu, and Ruth Vanita, eds. *In Search of Answers: Indian Women's Voices from Manushi.* London: Zed Books, 1984.

Matsui, Yayori. *Women's Asia.* London: Zed Books, 1989.

Mohanty, Chandra Talpade, Ann Russo, and Lourdes Torres, eds. *Third World Women and the Politics of Feminism.* Indianapolis: Indiana University Press, 1991.

Moraga, Cherríe, and Gloria Anazaldúa, eds. *The Bridge Called My Back: Writings by Redical Women of Color.* New York: Kitchen Table, 1983.

Morgan, Robin, ed. *Sisterhood Is Global.* Garden City: Anchor Press/ Doubleday, 1984.

Romero, Oscar A. *Voice of the Voiceless.* Maryknoll, NY: Orbis Books, 1985.

Rosaldo, Michelle Zimbalist, and Louis Lamphere, eds. *Women, Culture and Society.* Stanford, CA: Stanford University Press, 1974.

Schaef, Anne Wilson. *Women's Reality: An Emerging Female System in a White Male Society.* San Francisco: Harper & Row, 1985.

Waters, Frank. *The Earp Brothers of Tombstone.* New York: Bramhall House, 1940.

Wee, Vivienne, and Noeleen Heyzer. *Gender, Poverty and Sustainable Development: Towards a Holistic Framework of Understanding and Action.* New York: UNDP Engender, 1995.

Woman's Studies Program of Rutgers University—New Brunswick. *Women, Culture and Society: A Reader.* Dubuque, IA: Kendall/Hunter Publishing Company, 1992.

Women in Politics and Decision-Making in the Late Twentieth Century: A United Nations Study. New York: United Nations Publications, 1994.

WOMEN AND WORK

Adams, Carol J., ed. *Ecofeminism and the Sacred.* New York: Continuum, 1993.

Afshar, Haleh, ed. *Women, Work, and Ideology in the Third World.* London: Tavistock Publications, 1985.

Alvarado, Elvia, with Medea Benjamin, ed. *Don't Be Afraid, Gringo: The Story of Elvia Alvarado.* San Francisco: Food First, 1987.

Barlet, Donald L., and James B. Steele. *America: What Went Wrong?* Kansas City: Andrews and McMeel, 1992.

Barnet, Richard J., and Ronald E. Muller. *Global Reach: The Power of the Multinational Corporations.* New York: Simon and Schuster, 1974.

Capeling-Alakija, Sharon. *Annual Report 1990 United Nations Development Fund for Women*. New York: UNIFEM, 1991.

Cavanagh, John, et al., eds. *Trading Freedom: How Free Trade Affects Our Lives, Work, and Environment*. San Francisco: The Institute for Food and Development Policy, 1992.

———. *From Debt To Development: Alternatives to the International Debt Crisis*. Washington, DC: The Institute for Policy Studies, 1985.

Daly, Herman E., and John B. Cobb, Jr. *For the Common Good*. Boston: Beacon Press, 1989.

George, Susan. *A Fate Worse Than Debt: The World Financial Crisis and the Poor*. New York: Grove Press, 1988.

Henderson, Hazel. *Paradigms in Progress*. Indianapolis: Knowledge Systems, 1991.

Henry, Sarah. "Labor & Lace." *San Francisco Chronicle*, September 5, 1993, Sec. This World, p. 9, col. 1.

Karmel, Rachael. *The Gloval Factory: Analysis and Action for a New Economic Era*. American Friends Service Committee, 1990.

Khandker, Shahidur R., Baqui Khalily, and Zahed Khan. *Grameen Bank: Performance and Sustainability*. Washington, DC: The World Bank, n.d.

Kodish, Marilyn, ed. *Pearls of Bangladesh: The Workers and Borrowers of Grameen Bank*. Washington, DC: Results Educational Fund. 1993.

Lam, Wing. "Editorial: Workers' Centers and the New Labor Movement." CSWA News: The Voice of Chinese American Workers (Summer 1994) Vol. 4, Issue 1, p. 6.

Lappe, Frances Moore, and Joseph Collins. *World Hunger: Twelve Myths*. New York: Grove Press, 1986.

Mies, Maria, and Vandana Shiva. *Ecofeminism*. London: Zed Books, 1993.

Nelson-Pallmeyer, Jack. *Brave New World Order*. Maryknoll, NY: Orbis Books, 1992.

Owensby, Walter L. *Economics for Prophets: A Primer on Concepts, Realities, and Values in Our Economic System*. Grand Rapids, MI: William B. Eerdmans Publishing, 1988.

Poor in the World Economy. Geneva, Switzerland: World Council of Churches,1989

Potter, George Ann. *Dialogue on Debt: Alternative Analyses and Solutions*. Washington, DC: The Center of Concern, 1988.

Schumacher, E.F. *Small Is Beautiful*. New York: Harper & Row, 1973.

Sen, Gita, and Caren Grown. *Development, Crises, and Alternative Visions: Third World Women's Perspectives*. New York: Monthly Review Press, 1987.

Shiva, Vandana, ed. *Close to Home: Women Reconnect Ecology, Health and Development Worldwide*. Philadelphia: New Society Publishers, 1994.

———. *Staying Alive: Women, Ecology and Development*. London: Zed Books, 1989.

Son, Dug-Soo, and Mi-Kyung Lee. *My Mother's Name is Worry*, Christian Institute for the Study of Justice and Development, 1983.

Vickers, Jeanne, ed. *Women and The World Economic Crisis*. London: Zed Books, 1991.

Ward, Kathryn, ed. *Women Workers and Global Restructuring*. Ithaca, NY: ILR Press, Cornell University, 1990.

Waring, Marilyn. *If Women Counted: A New Feminist Economics*. San Francisco: Harper & Row, 1988.

Women and Informal Sector: Their Contribution, Vulnerability and Future. New York: United Nations Educational Scientific and Cultural Organization, 1992.

WOMEN AND PEACE

Barrett, Jane, Aneene Dawber, Barbara Klugman, Ingrid Obery, Jennifer Shindler, and Joanne Yawitch. *South African Women on the Move*. London: Zed Books, 1985.

Barton, Carol. *Women and the Gulf War*. New York: Church Women United, 1991.

Coerr, Eleanor. *Sadako*. New York: G.P. Putnam's Sons, 1993.

Detainees' Parents Support Committee. *Cries of Freedom: Women in Detention in South Africa*. London: Catholic Institute for International Relations, 1988.

Freire, Paulo, *Pedagogy of the Oppressed*. New York: Continuum, 1986.

Gelb, Joyce, and Marian Lief Palley. *Women and Public Policies*. Princeton, NJ: Princeton University Press, 1982.

Golden, Renny. *The Hour of the Poor, The Hour of Women: Salvadoran Women Speak*. New York: Crossroad, 1991.

Goodwin, June. *Cry Amandla! South African Women and the Question of Power*. New York: Holmes & Meier, 1984.

Grant, Rebecca, and Kathleen Newland. *Gender and International Relations*. Bloomington: Indiana University Press, 1991.

International Defence and Aid Fund for Southern Africa. *Women Under Apartheid*. London: United Nations Centre Against Apartheid, 1981.

Keen, Sam. *Faces of the Enemy: Reflections of the Hostile Imagination*. San Francisco: Harper & Row, 1986.

McAllister, Pam. *You Can't Kill the Spirit*. Philadelphia: New Society Publishers, 1988.

———. *Reweaving the Web of Life: Feminism and Nonviolence*. Philadelphia: New Society Publishers, 1982.

Nelson, Barbara J., and Najma Chowdhury. *Women and Politics Worldwide*. New Haven, CT: Yale University Press, 1994.

Oracion, Levi. *Ideologies and People's Struggles for Justice, Freedom, and Peace*. Geneva, Switzerland: World Council of Churches, 1988.

Randall, Margaret. *Women in Cuba: Twenty Years Later*. New York: Smyrna Press, 1981.

Roth, Katherine. "An Egyptian Feminist's Fight to Protect Hard-Won Gains." *San Francisco Chronicle*, September 23, 1991, Sec. Briefing.

Samuel, Shirin. *Fellowship of the Least Coin: Global Movement of Prayer for Peace, Justice and Reconciliation*. Multan, Pakistan: Fellowship of the Least Coin, n.d.

Weir, Ben, and Carol Weir, with Dennis Benson. *Hostage Bound Hostage Free*. Philadelphia: Westminster Press, 1987.

Wolf, Naomi. *Fire with Fire: The New Female Power and How to Use It*. New York: Fawcett Columbine, 1994.

Young, Iris Marion. *Justice and the Politics of Difference*. Princeton, NJ: Princeton University Press, 1990.

WOMEN AND VIOLENCE

Braswell, Linda. *Quest for Respect: A Guide to Healing for Survivors of Rape*. Ventura, CA: Pathfinder Publishing, 1989.

Equal Rights For Women (and Girls). *Women 2000*, No.3, 1992. Vienna, Austria: Division fo the Advancement of Women, Centre for Social Development and Humanitarian Affairs, 1992.

Giles-Sims, Jean. *Wife Battering: A Systems Theory Approach*. New York: The Guilford Press, 1983.

Gordon, Margaret T., and Stephanie Riger. *The Female Fear*. New York: Free Press, 1989.

Holden, Peter, Jurgen Horlemann, and Georg Friedrich Pfafflin. *Tourism Prostitution Development: Documentation*. Bangkok, Thailand: Ecumenical Coalition on Third World Tourism, 1985.

Jones, Ann. *Next Time, She'll Be Dead: Battering and How to Stop It*. Boston: Beacon Press, 1994.

Justice for Women Committee. *Myths and Facts about Rape and Battering*. Louisville, KY: Presbyterian Church (USA), n.d.

Langan, Patrick A., and Christopher A. Innes. *Prevent Domestic Violence against Women*. Washington, DC: U.S. Department of Justice, 1986.

Levy, Barrie, ed. *Dating Violence: Young Women in Danger*. Seattle, WA: Seal Press, 1991.

Martin, Laura. *A Life Without Fear: A Guide to Preventing Sexual Assault*. Nashville, TN: Rutledge Hill Press, 1992.

McGuire, Leslie. *Women Today Victims*. Vero Beach, FL: The Rourke Corporation, 1991.

National Victim Center and Crime Victims Research and Treatment Center. *Rape in America: A Report to the Nation*. Arlington, VA: National Victim Center, 1992.

O'Grady, Ron. *Children in Prostitution: Victims of Tourism in Asia*. Bangkok, Thailand: End Child Prostitution in Asian Tourism, 1991.

Pescatello, Ann, ed. *Female and Male in Latin America*. Pittsburgh: University of Pittsburgh Press, 1973.

Roy, Maria, ed. *The Abusive Partner: An Analysis of Domestic Battering*. New York: Van Nostrand Reinhold Company, 1982.

Saadawi, Nawal el. *The Hidden Face of Eve: Women in the Arab World*. London: Zed Books, 1980.

Samora, Julian, ed. *La Raza: Forgotten Americans*. Notre Dame, IN: University of Notre Dame Press, 1966.

Srisang, Koson. *Caught in Modern Slavery: Tourism and Child Prostitution in Asia*. Bangkok, Thailand: The Ecumenical Coalition on Third World Tourism, 1991.

Tamez, Elsa. *Against Machismo*. Oak Park, IL: Meyer Stone Books, 1987.

UNICEF. *The Progress of Nations*. New York: UNICEF House, 1994.

UNICEF. *The State of the World's Children: 1996*. New York: Oxford University Press, 1996.

Zorza, Joan. *The Gender Bias Committee's Domestic Violence Study: Important Recommendations and First Steps*. Boston: Boston Bar J.4, 13, July/August 1989.

WOMEN AND RELIGION

By Our Lives: Stories of Women Today and in the Bible. Geneva, Switzerland: World Council of Churches, 1985.

Clark, Don. *Loving Someone Gay*. New York: NAL-Dutton, 1978.

Eck, Diana L., and Devaki Jain. *Speaking of Faith: Global Perspective on Women Religion and Social Change*. Philadelphia: New Society Publishers, 1987.

Ecumenical Decade 1988–1998, Churches in Solidarity with Women: Prayers and Poems, Songs and Stories. Geneva, Switzerland: World Council of Churches, 1988.

Esquivel, Julia. *Threatened with Resurrection: Prayers and Poems from An Exiled Guatemalan*. Elgin, IL: The Brethren Press, 1982.

Fabella, Virginia, and Mercy Amba Oduyoye, eds. *With Passion and Compassion: Third World Women Doing Theology*. Maryknoll, NY: Orbis Books, 1988.

Faldamez, Pablo. *Faith of a People: The Life of a Basic Christian Community in El Salvador*. Maryknoll, NY: Orbis Books, 1986.

Fiorenza, Elisabeth Schussler. *In Memory of Her*. New York: Crossroad, 1985.

Fischer, Kathleen. *Women at the Well*. New York: Paulist Press, 1988.

Gutiérrez, Gistavo. *A Theology of Liberation*. Maryknoll, NY: Orbis Books, 1973.

Haddad, Yvonne Yazbeck, and Ellison Banks Findly, eds. *Women, Religion, and Social Change*. Albany, NY: State University of New York Press, 1985.

Isasi-Diaz, Ada Maria, and Yolanda Tatango. *Hispanic Women Prophetic Voice in the Church: Toward a Hispanic Women's Liberation Theology*. San Franciso: Harper and Row, 1988.

King, Ursula, ed. *Feminist Theology from the Third World*. Maryknoll, NY: Orbis Books, 1994.

————. *Women in the World's Religions: Past and Present*. New York: Paragon House, 1987.

Mollenkott, Virginia Ramey, ed. *Women of Faith in Dialogue*. New York: Crossroad, 1987.

Oduyoye, Mercy Amba. *Hearing and Knowing: Theological Reflections on Christianity in Africa*. Maryknoll, NY: Orbis Books, 1986.

Oduyoye, Mercy Amba, and Musimbi R. A. Kanyoro, eds. *The Will to Arise: Women, Traditions, and the Church in Africa*. Maryknoll, NY: Orbis Books, 1992.

Reading the Bible as Asian Women. Singapore: Christian Conference of Asia (Women's Concerns Unit), 1953.

Robins, Wendy S. *Through the Eyes of a Woman*. London: World YWCA, 1986.

Russell, Letty m., Kwok Pui-lan, Ada María Isasi-Díaz, and Katie Geneva Cannon. *Inheriting Our Mothers' Gardens: Feminist Theology in Third World Perspective*. Louisville, KY: Westminster Press, 1988.

Schmidt, Alvin John. *Veiled and Silenced: How Culture Shaped Sexist Theology*. Macon, GA: Mercer University Press, 1989.

Sharma, Arvind, ed. *Today's Women in World Religions*. Albany, NY: State University of New York Press, 1994.

————. *Women in World Religions*. Albany, NY: State University of New York Press, 1987.

Spretnak, Charlene, ed. *The Politics of Women's Spirituality: Essays on the Rise of Spiritual Power Within the Feminist Movement*. Garden City: AnchorPress/Doubleday,1982

Torres, Sergio, and John Eagleson, eds. *The Challenge of Basic Christian Communities*. Maryknoll, NY: Orbis Books, 1982.

von Wartenberg-Potter, Bärbel. *We Will Not Hang Our Harps on the Willows: Global Sisterhood and God's Song*. Oak Park. IL: Meyer Stone Books,1988.

Young, Serinity, ed. *An Anthology of Sacred Texts By and About Women*. New York: Crossroad, 1994.

Index

CERTIFICATE OF RECOGNITION

This Certifies That

Betty Boutell

Has completed Plan _____ IV _____ of

THE READING PROGRAM OF
UNITED METHODIST WOMEN

And is hereby awarded this certificate by

Ann Arbor District

Presented on the _____ 3rd _____ day of _____ October _____ 1998

Jan Olar
District Reading Coordinator

Joyce L. Middleton
District President